Rubáiyát of Omar Khayyám
THE ASTRONOMER-POET OF PERSIA

Translated into English Verse
by Edward FitzGerald

*Special Facsimile Edition
of the first edition of 1859*

*With contemporary computer-generated
typesetting of the first, second
and fifth editions*

Omar Khayyám's haunting, timeless verses were translated into English by Edward FitzGerald and first published in 1859. That first edition is presented here in facsimile, accompanied by computer-generated typesetting of the later editions, providing a 'complete edition'.

Persian astronomer-poet Omar Khayyám, writing nearly a thousand years ago, picks a path through life's uncertainties, musing on fate, transience and mortality, urging his reader to live in the moment and find joy in simple, everyday pleasures.

OTHER BOOKS BY KEITH SEDDON

Epictetus: The Discourses, Handbook and Fragments
[forthcoming]
The Stoic Fragments of Epictetus [forthcoming]
An Outline of Cynic Philosophy: Antisthenes of Athens and Diogenes of Sinope in Diogenes Laertius Book Six (with C. D. Yonge)
A Summary of Stoic Philosophy: Zeno of Citium in Diogenes Laertius Book Seven (with C. D. Yonge)
Stoic Serenity: A Practical Course on Finding Inner Peace
Epictetus' Handbook and the Tablet of Cebes: Guides to Stoic Living
Lao Tzu: Tao Te Ching
Learning the Tao: Chuang Tzu as Teacher
Tractatus Philosophicus Tao: A short treatise on the Tao Te Ching of Lao Tzu
Time: A Philosophical Treatment

TIMELESS WISDOM SERIES
Edited by Keith Seddon

Rubáiyát of Omar Khayyám: The First, Second, and Fifth Editions (With *AN ANALYSIS* by Edward Heron-Allen)
Precepts and Teachings of Ancient Egypt: The Wisdom of Ptah-Hotep and Amenemope
Dhammapada or Path of Virtue

SEE ALSO

Rubáiyát of Omar Khayyám: Illustrated First Edition

Rubáiyát of Omar Khayyám

THE ASTRONOMER-POET OF PERSIA

Translated into English Verse
by
Edward FitzGerald

*Special Facsimile Edition
of the first edition of 1859*

With contemporary computer-generated
typesetting of the first, second
and fifth editions

Edited by Keith Seddon

LULU

Rubáiyát of Omar Khayyám, Translated into English Verse by Edward FitzGerald, was first published in 1859, and subsequent editions appeared in 1868, 1872, 1879, and 1889.

This new facsimile edition of the *Rubáiyát*,
first published 2010
by Lulu
www.lulu.com
including the first edition of 1859, the second edition of 1868, and the fifth edition of 1889 (which is essentially the same as the previous third and fourth editions, containing only minor amendments indicated in footnotes).

© 2010 Keith Seddon

Typeset in Iowan Old Style 10/14

All rights reserved. No part of this book may be reprinted or reproduced or utilised in any form or by any electronic, mechanical, or other means, now known or hereafter invented, including photocopying and recording, or in any information storage or retrieval system, without permission in writing from the publisher.

ISBN 978–1–4457–5638–7 (hardback)
ISBN 978–1–4457–5637–0 (paperback)

One Moment in Annihilation's Waste,
One Moment, of the Well of Life to taste—
    The Stars are setting and the Caravan
Starts for the Dawn of Nothing—Oh, make haste!

RUBÁIYÁT

OF

OMAR KHAYYÁM,

THE ASTRONOMER-POET OF PERSIA.

Translated into English Verse.

LONDON:
BERNARD QUARITCH,
CASTLE STREET, LEICESTER SQUARE.
1859.

G. NORMAN, PRINTER, MAIDEN LANE, COVENT GARDEN, LONDON.

OMAR KHAYYÁM,

THE

ASTRONOMER-POET OF PERSIA.

OMAR KHAYYÁM was born at Naishápúr in Khorassán in the latter half of our Eleventh, and died within the First Quarter of our Twelfth, Century. The slender Story of his Life is curiously twined about that of two others very considerable Figures in their Time and Country: one of them, Hasan al Sabbáh, whose very Name has lengthen'd down to us as a terrible Synonym for Murder: and the other (who also tells the Story of all Three) Nizám al Mulk, Vizyr to Alp the Lion and Malik Shah, Son and Grandson of Toghrul Beg the Tartar, who had wrested Persia from the feeble Successor of Mahmúd the Great, and founded that Seljukian Dynasty which finally roused Europe into the Crusades. This Nizám al Mulk, in his *Wasýat*—or *Testament*—which he wrote and left as a Memorial for future Statesmen—relates the following, as quoted in the Calcutta Review, No. 59, from Mirkhond's History of the Assassins.

"'One of the greatest of the wise men of Khorassan was
'the Imám Mowaffak of Naishápur, a man highly honoured
'and reverenced,—may God rejoice his soul; his illustrious
'years exceeded eighty-five, and it was the universal belief
'that every boy who read the Koran or studied the tradi-
'tions in his presence, would assuredly attain to honour and
'happiness. For this cause did my father send me from
'Tús to Naishápur with Abd-u-samad, the doctor of law,
'that I might employ myself in study and learning under
'the guidance of that illustrious teacher. Towards me he
'ever turned an eye of favour and kindness, and as his pupil
'I felt for him extreme affection and devotion, so that I
'passed four years in his service. When I first came there,
'I found two other pupils of mine own age newly arrived,
'Hakim Omar Khayyám, and the ill-fated Ben Sabbáh.
'Both were endowed with sharpness of wit and the highest
'natural powers; and we three formed a close friendship
'together. When the Imám rose from his lectures, they
'used to join me, and we repeated to each other the lessons
'we had heard. Now Omar was a native of Naishápur,
'while Hasan Ben Sabbah's father was one Ali, a man of
'austere life and practice, but heretical in his creed and
'doctrine. One day Hasan said to me and to Khayyám, 'It
'is a universal belief that the pupils of the Imám Mowaffak
'will attain to fortune. Now, even if we *all* do not attain
'thereto, without doubt one of us will; what then shall be
'our mutual pledge and bond?' We answered 'Be it
'what you please.' 'Well,' he said, 'let us make a vow,
'that to whomsoever this fortune falls, he shall share it
'equally with the rest, and reserve no pre-eminence for him-

' self.' ' Be it so,' we both replied, and on these terms we ' mutually pledged our words. Years rolled on, and I went ' from Khorassan to Transoxiana, and wandered to Ghazni ' and Cabul; and when I returned, I was invested with ' office, and rose to be administrator of affairs during the ' Sultanate of Sultan Alp Arslán.' "

"He goes on to state, that years passed by, and both his old school-friends found him out, and came and claimed a share in his good fortune, according to the school-day vow. The Vizier was generous and kept his word. Hasan demanded a place in the government, which the Sultan granted at the Vizier's request; but discontented with a gradual rise, he plunged into the maze of intrigue of an oriental court, and, failing in a base attempt to supplant his benefactor, he was disgraced and fell. After many mishaps and wanderings, Hasan became the head of the Persian sect of the *Ismailians*,—a party of fanatics who had long murmured in obscurity, but rose to an evil eminence under the guidance of his strong and evil will. In A. B. 1090, he seized the castle of Alamút, in the province of Rúdbar, which lies in the mountainous tract, south of the Caspian sea; and it was from this mountain home he obtained that evil celebrity among the Crusaders as the OLD MAN OF THE MOUNTAINS, and spread terror through the Mohammedan world; and it is yet disputed whether the word *Assassin*, which they have left in the language of modern Europe as their dark memorial, is derived from the *hashish*, or opiate of hemp-leaves (the Indian *bhang,*) with which they maddened themselves to the sullen pitch of oriental desperation, or from the name of the founder of the dynasty, whom we have seen in his quiet collegiate days, at Naishápur. One of the countless victims of the Assassin's dagger was Nizám-ul-Mulk himself, the old school-boy friend."

" Omar Khayyám also came to the Vizier to claim his share; but not to ask for title or office. 'The greatest boon 'you can confer on me,' he said, 'is to let me live in a 'corner under the shadow of your fortune, to spread wide 'the advantages of Science, and pray for your long life and 'prosperity.' The Vizier tells us, that, when he found Omar was really sincere in his refusal, he pressed him no further, but granted him a yearly pension of 1,200 *mithkáls* of gold, from the treasury of Naishápur."

" At Naishápur thus lived and died Omar Khayyám, 'busied,' adds the Vizier, 'in winning knowledge of every 'kind, and especially in Astronomy, wherein he attained to a 'very high pre-eminence. Under the Sultanate of Malik 'Shah, he came to Merv, and obtained great praise for his 'proficiency in science, and the Sultan showered favours 'upon him.'"

" When Malik Shah determined to reform the calendar, Omar was one of the eight learned men employed to do it; the result was the *Jaláli* era, (so called from *Jalal-ul-din*, one of the king's names,)—'a computation of time,' says Gibbon, 'which surpasses the Julian, and approaches the 'accuracy of the Gregorian style.' He is also the author of some astronomical tables, entitled 'Zíji-Malikshahí,' and the French have lately republished and translated an Arabic Treatise of his on Algebra."

" These severer Studies, and his Verses, which, though happily fewer than any Persian Poet's, and, though perhaps fugitively composed, the Result of no fugitive Emotion or Thought, are probably the Work and Event of his Life, leaving little else to record. Perhaps he liked a little Farming too, so often as he speaks of the ' Edge of the Tilth ' on which he loved to rest with his Diwán of Verse, his Loaf —and his Wine."

" His Takhallus or poetical name (Khayyám) signifies a Tent-maker, and he is said to have at one time exercised that trade, perhaps before Nizám-ul-Mulk's generosity raised him to independence. Many Persian poets similarly derive their names from their occupations ; thus we have Attár, ' a druggist,' Assar, ' an oil presser,' &c. (Though all these, like our Smiths, Archers, Millers, Fletchers, &c. may simply retain the Sirname of an hereditary calling.) Omar himself alludes to his name in the following whimsical lines :—

> ' Khayyám, who stitched the tents of science,
> Has fallen in grief's furnace and been suddenly burned
> The shears of Fate have cut the tent ropes of his life,
> And the broker of Hope has sold him for nothing !'

" We have only one more anecdote to give of his Life, and that relates to the close ; related in the anonymous preface which is sometimes prefixed to his poems ; it has been printed in the Persian in the appendix to Hyde's *Veterum Persarum Religio*, p. 499 ; and D'Herbelot alludes to it in his Bibliothéque, under *Khiam* :—*

---

* Though *he* attributes the story to a Khiam, " Philosophe Musulman qui a vécu en Odeur de Sainteté dans la Fin du premier et le Commencement du second Siècle," no part of which, except the " Philosophe," can apply to *our* Khayyám, who, however, may claim the Story as *his*, on the

'It is written in the chronicles of the ancients that this 'King of the Wise, Omar Khayyám, died at Naishápur in 'the year of the Hegira, 517 (A.D. 1123); in science he was 'unrivalled—the very paragon of his age. Khwájah Nizámi 'of Samarcand, who was one of his pupils, relates the follow-'ing story: I often used to hold conversations with my 'teacher, Omar Khayyám, in a garden; and one day he said 'to me, 'my tomb shall be in a spot, where the north wind 'may scatter roses over it.' I wondered at the words he 'spake, but I knew that his were no idle words. Years after, 'when I chanced to revisit Naishápur, I went to his final 'resting place, and lo! it was just outside a garden, and trees 'laden with fruit stretched their boughs over the garden 'wall, and dropped their flowers upon his tomb, so as the 'stone was hidden under them.'"

Thus far—without fear of Trespass—from the Calcutta Review.

Though the Sultan "shower'd Favours upon him," Omar's Epicurean Audacity of Thought and Speech caused him to be regarded askance in his own Time and Country. He is said to have been especially hated and dreaded by the Súfis, whose Practice he ridiculed, and whose Faith amounts to little more than his own when stript of the Mysticism and formal Compliment to Islamism which Omar would not hide under. Their Poets, including Háfiz, who are (with

---

Score of Rubáiyát, 77 and 78 of the present Version. The Rashness of the Words, according to D'Herbelot, consisted in being so opposed to those in the Korán: "No Man knows where he shall die."

the exception of Firdúsi) the most considerable in Persia, borrowed largely, indeed, of Omar's material, but turning it to a mystical Use more convenient to Themselves and the People they address'd ; a People quite as quick of Doubt as of Belief ; quite as keen of the Bodily Senses as of the Intellectual ; and delighting in a cloudy Element compounded of all, in which they could float luxuriously between Heaven and Earth, and this World and the Next, on the wings of a poetical expression, that could be recited indifferently whether at the Mosque or the Tavern. Omar was too honest of Heart as well as of Head for this. Having failed (however mistakenly) of finding any Providence but Destiny, and any World but This, he set about making the most of it ; preferring rather to soothe the Soul through the Senses into Acquiescence with Things as they were, than to perplex it with vain mortifications after what they *might be*. It has been seen that his Worldly Desires, however, were not exorbitant; and he very likely takes a humourous pleasure in exaggerating them above that Intellect in whose exercise he must have found great pleasure, though not in a Theological direction. However this may be, his Worldly Pleasures are what they profess to be without any Pretence at divine Allegory : his Wine is the veritable Juice of the Grape : his Tavern, where it was to be had : his Sáki, the Flesh and Blood that poured it out for him : all which, and where the Roses were in Bloom, was all he profess'd to want of this World or to expect of Paradise.

The Mathematic Faculty, too, which regulated his Fansy, and condensed his Verse to a Quality and Quantity unknown in Persian, perhaps in Oriental, Poetry, help'd by its very virtue perhaps to render him less popular with his countrymen. If the Greeks were Children in Gossip, what does Persian Literature imply but a *Second Childishness* of Garrulity ? And certainly if no *ungeometric* Greek was to enter Plato's School of Philosophy, no so unchastised a Persian should enter on the Race of Persian Verse, with its " fatal Facility " of running on long after Thought is winded! But Omar was not only the single Mathematician of his Country's Poets ; he was also of that older Time and stouter Temper, before the native Soul of Persia was quite broke by a foreign Creed as well as foreign Conquest. Like his great Predecessor Firdúsi, who was as little of a *Mystic ;* who scorned to use even a *Word* of the very language in which the New Faith came clothed ; and who was suspected, not of Omar's Irreligion indeed, but of secretly clinging to the ancient Fire-Religion of Zerdusht, of which so many of the Kings he sang were Worshippers.

For whatever Reason, however, Omar, as before said, has never been popular in his own Country, and therefore has been but charily transmitted abroad. The MSS. of his Poems, mutilated beyond the average Casualties of Oriental Transcription, are so rare in the East as scarce to have reacht Westward at all, in spite of all that Arms and Science have brought us. There is none at the India House, none at the Bibliothêque Imperiále of Paris. We know but of one in England ; No. 140 of the Ouseley MSS. at the Bodleian, written at Shiraz, A.D. 1460. This contains but 158 Rabáiyát. One in the Asiatic Society's Library of Calcutta, (of which we have a Copy) contains (and yet incomplete) 516, though swelled to that by all kinds of Repetition and

Corruption. So Von Hammer speaks of *his* Copy as containing about 200, while Dr. Sprenger catalogues the Lucknow MS. at double that Number. The Scribes, too, of the Oxford and Calcutta MSS. seem to do their Work under a sort of Protest ; each beginning with a Tetrastich (whether genuine or not) taken out of its alphabetic order; the Oxford with one of Apology ; the Calcutta with one of Execration too stupid for Omar's, even had Omar been stupid enough to execrate himself.*

The Reviewer, who translates the foregoing Particulars of Omar's Life, and some of his Verse into Prose, concludes by comparing him with Lucretius, both in natural Temper and Genius, and as acted upon by the Circumstances in which he lived. Both indeed men of subtle Intellect and high Imagination, instructed in Learning beyond their day, and of Hearts passionate for Truth and Justice ; who justly revolted from their Country's false Religion, and false, or foolish, Devotion to it ; but who yet fell short of replacing what they subverted by any such better *Hope* as others, upon whom no better *Faith* had dawned, had yet made a Law to themselves. Lucretius, indeed, with such material as Epicurus furnished, consoled himself with the construction of a Machine that needed no Constructor, and acting by a Law that implied no Lawgiver ; and so composing himself into a Stoical rather than Epicurean severity of Attitude, sat down to contemplate the mechanical Drama of the Universe of which he was part Actor ;

* " Since this Paper was written" (adds the Reviewer in a note) " we have met with a Copy of a very rare Edition, printed at Calcutta in 1836. This contains 438 Tetrastichs, with an Appendix containing 54 others not found in some MSS."

himself and all about him, (as in his own sublime Description of the Roman Theatre,) coloured with the lurid reflex of the Curtain that was suspended between them and the outer Sun. Omar, more desperate, or more careless, of any such laborious System as resulted in nothing more than hopeless Necessity, flung his own Genius and Learning with a bitter jest into the general Ruin which their insufficient glimpses only served to reveal ; and, yielding his Senses to the actual Rose and Vine, only *diverted* his thoughts by balancing ideal possibilities of Fate, Freewill, Existence and Annihilation ; with an oscillation that so generally inclined to the negative and lower side, as to make such Stanzas as the following exceptions to his general Philosophy—

> Oh, if my Soul can fling his Dust aside,
> And naked on the Air of Heaven ride,
>   Is't not a Shame, is't not a Shame for Him
> So long in this Clay Suburb to abide!
>
> Or is *that* but a Tent, where rests anon
> A Sultán to his Kingdom passing on,
>   And which the swarthy Chamberlain shall strike
> Then when the Sultán rises to be gone ?

With regard to the present Translation. The original Rubáiyát (as, missing an Arabic Guttural, these *Tetrastichs* are more musically called), are independent Stanzas, consisting each of four Lines of equal, though varied, Prosody, sometimes *all* rhyming, but oftener (as here attempted) the third line suspending the Cadence by which the last atones with the former Two. Something as in the Greek Alcaic, where the third line seems to lift and suspend the

Wave that falls over in the last. As usual with such kind of Oriental Verse, the Rubáiyát follow one another according to Alphabetic Rhyme—a strange Farrago of Grave and Gay. Those here selected are strung into something of an Eclogue, with perhaps a less than equal proportion of the " Drink and make-merry," which (genuine or not) recurs over-frequently in the Original. For Lucretian as Omar's Genius might be, he cross'd that darker Mood with much of Oliver de Basselin Humour. Any way, the Result is sad enough: saddest perhaps when most ostentatiously merry: any way, fitter to move Sorrow than Anger toward the old Tentmaker, who, after vainly endeavouring to unshackle his Steps from Destiny, and to catch some authentic Glimpse of TOMORROW, fell back upon TODAY (which has out-lasted so many Tomorrows!) as the only Ground he got to stand upon, however momentarily slipping from under his Feet.

RUBÁIYÁT

OF

OMAR KHAYYÁM OF NAISHÁPÚR.

I.

Awake! for Morning in the Bowl of Night
Has flung the Stone that puts the Stars to Flight:[1]
 And Lo! the Hunter of the East has caught
The Sultán's Turret in a Noose of Light.

II.

Dreaming when Dawn's Left Hand was in the sky[2]
I heard a Voice within the Tavern cry,
 "Awake, my Little ones, and fill the Cup
"Before Life's Liquor in its Cup be dry."

III.

And, as the Cock crew, those who stood before
The Tavern shouted—"Open then the Door!
 "You know how little while we have to stay,
"And, once departed, may return no more."

IV.

Now the New Year[3] reviving old Desires,
The thoughtful Soul to Solitude retires,
   Where the WHITE HAND OF MOSES on the Bough
Puts out,[4] and Jesus from the Ground suspires.

V.

Irám indeed is gone with all its Rose,[5]
And Jamshýd's Sev'n-ring'd Cup where no one knows;
   But still the Vine her ancient Ruby yields,
And still a Garden by the Water blows.

VI.

And David's Lips are lock't; but in divine
High piping Péhlevi,[6] with "Wine! Wine! Wine!
   "*Red* Wine!"—the Nightingale cries to the Rose
That yellow Cheek[7] of her's to'incarnadine.

VII.

Come, fill the Cup, and in the Fire of Spring
The Winter Garment of Repentance fling:
   The Bird of Time has but a little way
To fly—and Lo! the Bird is on the Wing.

VIII.

And look—a thousand Blossoms with the Day
Woke—and a thousand scatter'd into Clay:
   And this first Summer Month that brings the Rose
Shall take Jamshýd and Kaikobád away.

IX.

But come with old Khayyám, and leave the Lot
Of Kaikobád and Kaikhosrú forgot :
   Let Rustum lay about him as he will,[8]
Or Hátim Tai cry Supper—heed them not.

X.

With me along some Strip of Herbage strown
That just divides the desert from the sown,
   Where name of Slave and Sultán scarce is known,
And pity Sultán Máhmúd on his Throne.

XI.

Here with a Loaf of Bread beneath the Bough,
A Flask of Wine, a Book of Verse—and Thou
   Beside me singing in the Wilderness—
And Wilderness is Paradise enow.

XII.

" How sweet is mortal Sovranty ! "—think some :
Others—" How blest the Paradise to come!"
   Ah, take the Cash in hand and wave the Rest ;
Oh, the brave Music of a *distant* Drum ![9]

XIII.

Look to the Rose that blows about us—" Lo,
" Laughing," she says, " into the World I blow :
   " At once the silken Tassel of my Purse
" Tear, and its Treasure[10] on the Garden throw."

XIV.

The Worldly Hope men set their Hearts upon
Turns Ashes—or it prospers; and anon,
    Like Snow upon the Desert's dusty Face
Lightning a little Hour or two—is gone.

XV.

And those who husbanded the Golden Grain,
And those who flung it to the Winds like Rain,
    Alike to no such aureate Earth are turn'd
As, buried once, Men want dug up again.

XVI.

Think, in this batter'd Caravanserai
Whose Doorways are alternate Night and Day,
    How Sultán after Sultán with his Pomp
Abode his Hour or two, and went his way.

XVII.

They say the Lion and the Lizard keep
The Courts where Jamshýd gloried and drank deep :[11]
    And Bahrám, that great Hunter—the Wild Ass
Stamps o'er his Head, and he lies fast asleep.

XVIII.

I sometimes think that never blows so red
The Rose as where some buried Cæsar bled ;
    That every Hyacinth the Garden wears
Dropt in its Lap from some once lovely Head.

XIX.

And this delightful Herb whose tender Green
Fledges the River's Lip on which we lean—
  Ah, lean upon it lightly! for who knows
From what once lovely Lip it springs unseen!

XX.

Ah, my Belovéd, fill the Cup that clears
To-DAY of past Regrets and future Fears—
  To-morrow?—Why, To-morrow I may be
Myself with Yesterday's Sev'n Thousand Years.[12]

XXI.

Lo! some we loved, the loveliest and best
That Time and Fate of all their Vintage prest,
  Have drunk their Cup a Round or two before,
And one by one crept silently to Rest.

XXII.

And we, that now make merry in the Room
They left, and Summer dresses in new Bloom,
  Ourselves must we beneath the Couch of Earth
Descend, ourselves to make a Couch—for whom?

XXIII.

Ah, make the most of what we yet may spend,
Before we too into the Dust descend;
  Dust into Dust, and under Dust, to lie,
Sans Wine, sans Song, sans Singer, and—sans End!

XXIV.

Alike for those who for To-day prepare,
And those that after a To-morrow stare,
   A Muezzín from the Tower of Darkness cries
"Fools! your Reward is neither Here nor There!"

XXV.

Why, all the Saints and Sages who discuss'd
Of the Two Worlds so learnedly, are thrust
   Like foolish Prophets forth; their Words to Scorn
Are scatter'd, and their Mouths are stopt with Dust.

XXVI.

Oh, come with old Khayyám, and leave the Wise
To talk; one thing is certain, that Life flies;
   One thing is certain, and the Rest is Lies;
The Flower that once has blown for ever dies.

XXVII.

Myself when young did eagerly frequent
Doctor and Saint, and heard great Argument
   About it and about: but evermore
Came out by the same Door as in I went.

XXVIII.

With them the Seed of Wisdom did I sow,
And with my own hand labour'd it to grow:
   And this was all the Harvest that I reap'd—
"I came like Water, and like Wind I go."

XXIX.

Into this Universe, and *why* not knowing,
Nor *whence*, like Water willy-nilly flowing:
   And out of it, as Wind along the Waste,
I know not *whither*, willy-nilly blowing.

XXX.

What, without asking, hither hurried *whence* ?
And, without asking, *whither* hurried hence !
   Another and another Cup to drown
The Memory of this Impertinence !

XXXI.

Up from Earth's Centre through the Seventh Gate
I rose, and on the Throne of Saturn sate,[13]
   And many Knots unravel'd by the Road ;
But not the Knot of Human Death and Fate.

XXXII.

There was a Door to which I found no Key :
There was a Veil past which I could not see :
   Some little Talk awhile of ME and THEE
There seemed—and then no more of THEE and ME.[15]

XXXIII.

Then to the rolling Heav'n itself I cried,
Asking, " What Lamp had Destiny to guide
   " Her little Children stumbling in the Dark ?"
And—" A blind Understanding !" Heav'n replied.

XXXIV.

Then to this earthen Bowl did I adjourn
My Lip the secret Well of Life to learn :
  And Lip to Lip it murmur'd—" While you live
" Drink !—for once dead you never shall return."

XXXV.

I think the Vessel, that with fugitive
Articulation answer'd, once did live,
  And merry-make ; and the cold Lip I kiss'd
How many Kisses might it take—and give !

XXXVI.

For in the Market-place, one Dusk of Day,
I watch'd the Potter thumping his wet Clay :
  And with its all obliterated Tongue
It murmur'd—" Gently, Brother, gently, pray!"

XXXVII.

Ah, fill the Cup :—what boots it to repeat
How Time is slipping underneath our Feet :
  Unborn TO-MORROW, and dead YESTERDAY,
Why fret about them if TO-DAY be sweet !

XXXVIII.

One Moment in Annihilation's Waste,
One Moment, of the Well of Life to taste—
  The Stars are setting and the Caravan
Starts for the Dawn of Nothing[16]—Oh, make haste !

XXXIX.

How long, how long, in infinite Pursuit
Of This and That endeavour and dispute ?
   Better be merry with the fruitful Grape
Than sadden after none, or bitter, Fruit.

XL.

You know, my Friends, how long since in my House
For a new Marriage I did make Carouse :
   Divorced old barren Reason from my Bed,
And took the Daughter of the Vine to Spouse.

XLI.

For " Is" and " Is-NOT" though *with* Rule and Line,
And " UP-AND-DOWN" *without*, I could define,[14]
   I yet in all I only cared to know,
Was never deep in anything but—Wine.

XLII.

And lately, by the Tavern Door agape,
Came stealing through the Dusk an Angel Shape
   Bearing a Vessel on his Shoulder ; and
He bid me taste of it ; and 'twas—the Grape !

XLIII.

The Grape that can with Logic absolute
The Two-and-Seventy jarring Sects[17] confute :
   The subtle Alchemist that in a Trice
Life's leaden Metal into Gold transmute.

XLIV.

The mighty Mahmúd, the victorious Lord,
That all the misbelieving and black Horde[18]
  Of Fears and Sorrows that infest the Soul
Scatters and slays with his enchanted Sword.

XLV.

But leave the Wise to wrangle, and with me
The Quarrel of the Universe let be :
  And, in some corner of the Hubbub coucht,
Make Game of that which makes as much of Thee.

XLVI.

For in and out, above, about, below,
'Tis nothing but a Magic Shadow-show,
  Play'd in a Box whose Candle is the Sun,
Round which we Phantom Figures come and go.[19]

XLVII.

And if the Wine you drink, the Lip you press,
End in the Nothing all Things end in—Yes—
  Then fancy while Thou art, Thou art but what
Thou shalt be—Nothing—Thou shalt not be less.

XLVIII.

While the Rose blows along the River Brink,
With old Khayyám the Ruby Vintage drink :
  And when the Angel with his darker Draught
Draws up to Thee—take that, and do not shrink.

XLIX.

'Tis all a Chequer-board of Nights and Days
Where Destiny with Men for Pieces plays :
   Hither and thither moves, and mates, and slays,
And one by one back in the Closet lays.

L.

The Ball no Question makes of Ayes and Noes,
But Right or Left as strikes the Player goes ;
   And He that toss'd Thee down into the Field,
He knows about it all—HE knows—HE knows ![20]

LI.

The Moving Finger writes ; and, having writ,
Moves on : nor all thy Piety nor Wit
   Shall lure it back to cancel half a Line,
Nor all thy Tears wash out a Word of it.

LII.

And that inverted Bowl we call The Sky,
Whereunder crawling coop't we live and die,
   Lift not thy hands to *It* for help—for It
Rolls impotently on as Thou or I.

LIII.

With Earth's first Clay They did the Last Man's knead,
And then of the Last Harvest sow'd the Seed :
   Yea, the first Morning of Creation wrote
What the Last Dawn of Reckoning shall read.

LIV.

I tell Thee this—When, starting from the Goal,
Over the shoulders of the flaming Foal
    Of Heav'n Parwín and Mushtara they flung,[21]
In my predestin'd Plot of Dust and Soul

LV.

The Vine had struck a Fibre ; which about
If clings my Being—let the Súfi flout ;
    Of my Base Metal may be filed a Key,
That shall unlock the Door he howls without.

LVI.

And this I know : whether the one True Light,
Kindle to Love, or Wrathconsume me quite,
    One Glimpse of It within the Tavern caught
Better than in the Temple lost outright.

LVII.

Oh Thou, who didst with Pitfall and with Gin
Beset the Road I was to wander in,
    Thou wilt not with Predestination round
Enmesh me, and impute my Fall to Sin ?

LVIII.

Oh, Thou, who Man of baser Earth didst make,
And who with Eden didst devise the Snake ;
    For all the Sin wherewith the Face of Man
Is blacken'd, Man's Forgiveness give—and take !

* * * * * * * *

KÚZA-NÁMA.

LIX.

Listen again. One Evening at the Close
Of Ramazán, ere the better Moon arose,
  In that old Potter's Shop I stood alone
With the clay Population round in Rows.

LX.

And, strange to tell, among that Earthen Lot
Some could articulate, while others not:
  And suddenly one more impatient cried—
"Who *is* the Potter, pray, and who the Pot?"

LXI.

Then said another—"Surely not in vain
"My Substance from the common Earth was ta'en,
  "That He who subtly wrought me into Shape
"Should stamp me back to common Earth again."

LXII.

Another said—"Why, ne'er a peevish Boy,
"Would break the Bowl from which he drank in Joy;
  "Shall He that *made* the Vessel in pure Love
"And Fansy, in an after Rage destroy!"

LXIII.

None answer'd this ; but after Silence spake
A Vessel of a more ungainly Make :
  " They sneer at me for leaning all awry ;
" What ! did the Hand then of the Potter shake ?"

LXIV.

Said one—" Folks of a surly Tapster tell,
" And daub his Visage with the Smoke of Hell ;
  " They talk of some strict Testing of us—Pish !
" He's a Good Fellow, and 'twill all be well."

LXV.

Then said another with a long-drawn Sigh,
" My Clay with long oblivion is gone dry :
  " But, fill me with the old familiar Juice,
" Methinks I might recover by-and-bye !"

LXVI.

So while the Vessels one by one were speaking,
One spied the little Crescent all were seeking :
  And then they jogg'd each other, " Brother ! Brother !
" Hark to the Porter's Shoulder-knot a-creaking !"

*   *   *   *   *   *   *   *

LXVII.

Ah, with the Grape my fading Life provide,
And wash my Body whence the Life has died,
   And in a Windingsheet of Vine-leaf wrapt,
So bury me by some sweet Garden-side.

LXVIII.

That ev'n my buried Ashes such a Snare
Of Perfume shall fling up into the Air,
   As not a True Believer passing by
But shall be overtaken unaware.

LXIX.

Indeed the Idols I have loved so long
Have done my Credit in Men's Eye much wrong:
   Have drown'd my Honour in a shallow Cup,
And sold my Reputation for a Song.

LXX.

Indeed, indeed, Repentance oft before
I swore—but was I sober when I swore?
   And then and then came Spring, and Rose-in-hand
My thread-bare Penitence apieces tore.

LXXI.

And much as Wine has play'd the Infidel,
And robb'd me of my Robe of Honour—well,
   I often wonder what the Vintners buy
One half so precious as the Goods they sell.

LXXII.

Alas, that Spring should vanish with the Rose!
That Youth's sweet-scented Manuscript should close!
   The Nightingale that in the Branches sang,
Ah, whence, and whither flown again, who knows!

LXXIII.

Ah Love! could thou and I with Fate conspire
To grasp this sorry Scheme of Things entire,
   Would not we shatter it to bits—and then
Re-mould it nearer to the Heart's Desire!

LXXIV.

Ah, Moon of my Delight who know'st no wane,
The Moon of Heav'n is rising once again:
   How oft hereafter rising shall she look
Through this same Garden after me—in vain!

LXXV.

And when Thyself with shining Foot shall pass
Among the Guests Star-scatter'd on the Grass,
   And in thy joyous Errand reach the Spot
Where I made one—turn down an empty Glass!

TAMÁM SHUD.

NOTES.

[1] Flinging a Stone into the Cup was the Signal for "To Horse!" in the Desert.

[2] The "*False Dawn;*" *Subhi Kházib*, a transient Light on the Horizon about an hour before the *Subhi sádhik*, or True Dawn; a well known Phenomenon in the East. The Persians call the Morning Gray, or Dusk, "*Wolf-and-Sheep-While.*" "Almost at odds with, which is which."

[3] New Year. Beginning with the Vernal Equinox, it must be remembered; and (howsoever the old Solar Year is practically superseded by the clumsy *Lunar* Year that dates from the Mohammedan Hijra) still commemorated by a Festival that is said to have been appointed by the very Jamshyd whom Omar so often talks of, and whose yearly Calendar he helped to rectify.

"The sudden approach and rapid advance of the Spring," (says a late Traveller in Persia) "are very striking. Before the Snow is well off the Ground, the Trees burst into Blossom, and the Flowers start from the Soil. At *Now Rooz* (*their* New Year's Day) the Snow was lying in patches on the Hills and in the shaded Vallies, while the Fruit-trees in the Garden were budding beautifully, and green Plants and Flowers springing upon the Plains on every side—

' And on Old Hyem's Chin and icy Crown
' An odorous Chaplet of sweet Summer buds
' Is, as in mockery, set—'—

Among the Plants newly appear'd I recognized some old Acquaintances I had not seen for many a Year : among these, two varieties of the Thistle ; a coarse species of the Daisy like the Horse-gowan ; red and white Clover ; the Dock ; the blue Corn-flower ; and that vulgar Herb the Dandelion rearing its yellow crest on the Banks of the Watercourses." The Nightingale was not yet heard, for the Rose was not yet blown : but an almost identical Blackbird and Woodpecker helped to make up something of a North-country Spring.

[4] Exodus iv. 6 ; where Moses draws forth his Hand—not, according to the Persians, " *leprous as Snow*,"—but *white* as our May-Blossom in Spring perhaps ! According to them also the Healing Power of Jesus resided in his Breath.

[5] Irám, planted by King Schedad, and now sunk somewhere in the Sands of Arabia. Jamshyd's Seven-ring'd Cup was typical of the Seven Heavens, 7 Planets, 7 Seas, &c. and was a *Divining Cup*.

[6] *Péhlevi*, the old Heroic *Sanskit* of Persia. Háfiz also speaks of the Nightingale's *Péhlevi*, which did not change with the People's.

[7] I am not sure if this refers to the Red Rose looking sickly, or the Yellow Rose that ought to be Red ; Red, White, and Yellow Roses all common in Persia.

[8] Rustum, the " Hercules" of Persia, whose exploits are among the most celebrated in the Shah-náma. Hátim Tai, a well-known Type of Oriental Generosity.

[9] A Drum—beaten outside a Palace.

[10] That is, the Rose's Golden Centre.

[11] Persepolis : call'd also *Takht'i Jamshyd*—THE THRONE OF JAMSHYD, "*King-Splendid*," of the mythical *Peeshdádian* Dynasty, and supposed (with Shah-náma Authority) to have been founded and built by him, though others refer it to the Work of the Genie King, Ján Ibn Jann, who also built the Pyramids before the time of Adam. It is also called *Chehl-minar—Forty-column ;* which is Persian, probably, for *Column-countless ;* the Hall they adorned or supported with their Lotus Base and taurine Capital indicating double that Number, though now counted down to less than half by Earthquake and other Inroad. By whomsoever built, unquestionably the Monument of a long extinguished Dynasty and Mythology ; its Halls, Chambers and Galleries, inscribed with Arrow-head Characters, and sculptured with colossal, wing'd, half human Figures like those of Nimroud ; Processions of Priests and Warriors —(doubtful if any where a Woman)—and Kings sitting on Thrones or in Chariots, Staff or Lotus-flower in hand, and the *Ferooher*—Symbol of Existence—with his wing'd Globe, common also to Assyria and Ægypt—over their heads. All this, together with Aqueduct and Cistern, and other Appurtenance of a Royal Palace, upon a Terrace-platform, ascended by a double Flight of Stairs that may be gallop'd up, and cut out of and into the Rock-side of the *Koh'i Ráhmet, Mountain of Mercy,* where the old Fire-Worshiping Sovereigns are buried, and overlooking the Plain of Merdasht.

Persians, like some other People, it seems, love to write their own Names, with sometimes a Verse or two, on their Country's Monuments. Mr. Binning (from whose sensible Travels the foregoing Account is mainly condens't) found several such in Persepolis; in one Place a fine Line of Háfiz: in another "an original, no doubt," he says, "by no great Poet," however "right in his Sentiment." The Words somehow looked to us, and the "halting metre" sounded, familiar; and on looking back at last among the 500 Rubáyiát of the Calcutta Omar MS.—*there* it is: old Omar quoted by *one* of his Countrymen, and here turned into hasty Rhyme, at any rate—

> "This Palace that its Top to Heaven threw,
> And Kings their Forehead on its Threshold drew—
> I saw a Ring-dove sitting there alone,
> And ' Coo, Coo, Coo,' she cried, and ' Coo, Coo, Coo.' "

So as it seems the Persian speaks the English Ring-dove's *Péhlevi*, which is also articulate Persian for "Where?"

BAHRÁM GÚR—*Bahrám of the Wild Ass*, from his Fame in hunting it—a Sassanian Sovereign, had also his Seven Castles (like the King of Bohemia!) each of a different Colour: each with a Royal Mistress within side; each of whom recounts to Bahrám a Romance, according to one of the most famous Poems of Persia, written by Amír Khusraw; these Sevens also figuring (according to Eastern Mysticism) the Seven Heavens, and perhaps the Book itself that Eighth, into which the mystical Seven transcend, and within which they revolve. The Ruins of Three of these Towers are yet shown by the Peasantry; as also the Swamp in which Bahrám sunk, like the Master of Ravenswood, while pursuing his *Gúr*.

[12] A Thousand Years to each Planet.

[13] Saturn, Lord of the Seventh Heaven.

[14] A Laugh at his Mathematics perhaps.

[15] ME AND THEE; that is, some Dividual Existence or Personality apart from the Whole.

[16] The Caravan travelling by Night (after their New Year's Day of the Vernal Equinox) by command of Mohammed, I believe.

[17] The 72 Sects into which Islamism so soon split.

[18] This alludes to Mahmúd's Conquest of India and its swarthy Idolaters.

[19] *Fanúsi khiyál*, a Magic lanthorn still used in India; the cylindrical Interior being painted with various Figures, and so lightly poised and ventilated as to revolve round the Candle lighted within.

[20] A very mysterious Line in the original;

U dánad u dánad u dánad u ——

breaking off something like our Wood-pigeon's Note, which she is said to take up just where she left off.

[21] Parwín and Mushtara—The Pleiads and Jupiter.

[22] At the Close of the Fasting Month, Ramazán (which makes the Musulman unhealthy and unamiable), the first Glimpse of the New Moon (who rules their Division of the Year) is looked for with the utmost Anxiety, and hailed with all Acclamation. Then it is that the Porter's Knot may be heard toward the *Cellar*, perhaps. Old Omar has elsewhere a pretty Quatrain about this same Moon—

 " Be of Good Cheer—the sullen Month will die,
 " And a young Moon requite us by and bye:
 " Look how the Old one meagre, bent, and wan
 " With Age and Fast, is fainting from the Sky!"

FINIS.

30 MR 59

NOTE ON THE TEXTS

The text of the *Rubáiyát of Omar Khayyám* which appears above is the first edition published in London in 1859 by Bernard Quaritch,[1] replicating a copy which the publisher sent to the British Museum under the terms of the legal deposit obligation that all publishers in Britain are required to satisfy. On the reverse of the title page is the British Museum deposit stamp, and at the very end (on the page opposite, left) we find a date-stamp indicating 30 March 1859 as the date of receipt.

The texts following this Note are computer-generated typeset versions of the *Rubáiyát*, comprising

(a) the same first edition published by Bernard Quaritch, amending six typographical errors (correcting *wave* to *waive* in stanza 12, changing *Lightning* to *Lighting*

---

[1] Available as a scanned facsimile (along with other editions) at the Electronic Text Center, University of Virginia Library: http://etext.lib.virginia.edu/modeng/modengF.browse.html (scroll down to 'Fitzgerald, Edward'). The facsimile has been created by utilising various components from the facsimile copy issued in 1939 by Percy Lund, Humphries & Co. Ltd., printers of Bradford and London, and that which appears in A. J. Arberry, *The Romance of the Rubáiyát* (London: George Allen & Unwin, 1959), both of which are now in the public domain.

in stanza 14, changing *Man's* to *Man* in stanza 53, changing *Fansy* to *Fancy* in stanza 62,[2] correcting *Sanskit* to *Sanskrit* in note 6, and restoring the missing superscript reference to note 22 in the second line of stanza 66), but retaining *Wrathconsume* in stanza 56 (which all subsequent editions print as *Wrath-consume*[3]), along with

---

[2] That this amendment to *Fansy* is required is suggested by the traditional orthographical rendering of *fancy* earlier in stanza 47 as well as *Fancy* occurring in stanza 92 of the second edition. Though possibly the correction has been made the wrong way round, as *Fansy* with the 's' spelling occurs in FitzGerald's first edition Preface about Omar Khayyám, in the opening sentence of the paragraph that commences 'The Mathematic Faculty' on pages ix, above, and 36, below. Note, however, that FitzGerald uses only *fancy* and never *fansy* throughout his *Letters* (see William Aldis Wright, *Letters and Literary Remains of Edward FitzGerald*, vols 1–4 of 7, New York: Macmillan 1902–03).

[3] Many later reprints of the first edition mistakenly adopt a space, or sometimes an en-dash or an em-dash (*Wrath consume, Wrath – consume, Wrath—consume*), which change the meaning and disrupt the metre; and sometimes they retain the meaning by following the typography of later editions by use of a hyphen (*Wrath-consume*). Most of the reprints of the later editions stick to the hyphen, though some editors prefer a space—and one even bizarrely opts for an extra comma (*Wrath, consume*)—which again changes the meaning. En-dashes and em-dashes do not appear to have contaminated any reprints of the later editions (and there's a small mercy to be thankful for). One commentator thankfully remarks that FitzGerald's adoption of a hyphen in later editions confirms that *wrathconsume* is indeed a compound verb, meaning 'destroy by anger', and cannot have been a misprint in the first edition, as some editors appear to think (Daniel Karlin, ed., *Rubáiyát of*

other idiosyncratic spellings (such as *dropt, stopt, prest,* and others), and renumbering and putting into correct sequence endnotes 14, 15 and 16;

(b) the second edition (of 1868) as published in London in 1907 by Macmillan,[4] and

(c) the fifth edition (of 1889) as published in London in 1894 by Macmillan.[5]

In all three editions offered here, I have elected to change the Roman numerals that head each stanza for Arabic numerals, change double quotation marks for single quotation marks according to current British usage (adopted also in a number of *Rubáiyát* editions), and omit repeated quotation marks from new lines (observing the style of several editions, including the Macmillan editions mentioned above), which changes stanza 2 for instance, from this

> "Awake, my Little ones, and fill the Cup
> "Before Life's Liquor in its Cup be dry."

to this

> 'Awake, my Little ones, and fill the Cup
> Before Life's Liquor in its Cup be dry.'

Omar Khayyám, Oxford: Oxford University Press 2009, page 161).

[4] Accompanied by the first and the fifth editions, though the latter is mistakenly identified as the fourth edition: careful checking shows that the text in this publication is indeed the correct typography for the fifth edition.

[5] Accompanied by the first edition.

NOTE ON THE TEXTS

Edward Fitzgerald's Prefaces to the various editions—offering some observations on the life of Omar Khayyám, accompanied by some thoughts on the *Rubáiyát*—differ only slightly. The Preface to the first edition of 1859, commencing on page 29, includes my translation from French in the first footnote, corrects three errors, amending 'A. B. 1090' to 'A. D. 1090' on page 31, amending the reference to stanzas 77 and 78 to 67 and 68 in the footnote on page 34, and restoring a missing closing quotation mark before FitzGerald's parenthetical note about surnames on page 33. The idiosyncratic (or possibly erroneous) spelling of 'Sirname' in the same note has been retained. A number of further minor typographical emendations have also been included. The Preface to the second edition has been omitted, as this is essentially the the same as that carried forward to the third and fifth editions (but not the fourth), the main difference amounting to its quoting Nicolas's French text at somewhat greater length.

KEITH SEDDON, *Editor*
Hertfordshire, England
May 2010

RUBÁIYÁT
OF
OMAR KHAYYÁM

FIRST EDITION

1859

OMAR KHAYYÁM

THE

ASTRONOMER-POET OF PERSIA

OMAR KHAYYÁM was born at Naishápúr in Khorassán in the latter half of our Eleventh, and died within the First Quarter of our Twelfth, Century. The slender Story of his Life is curiously twined about that of two other very considerable Figures in their Time and Country: one of them, Hasan al Sabbáh, whose very Name has lengthen'd down to us as a terrible Synonym for Murder: and the other (who also tells the Story of all Three) Nizám al Mulk, Vizyr to Alp the Lion and Malik Shah, Son and Grandson of Toghrul Beg the Tartar, who had wrested Persia from the feeble Successor of Mahmúd the Great, and founded that Seljukian Dynasty which finally roused Europe into the Crusades. This Nizám al Mulk, in his *Wasýat*—or *Testament*—which he wrote and left as a Memorial for future Statesmen—relates the following, as quoted in the Calcutta Review, No. 59, from Mirkhond's History of the Assassins.

"'One of the greatest of the wise men of Khorassan was the Imám Mowaffak of Naishápur, a man highly honoured and reverenced,—may God rejoice his soul; his illustrious years exceeded eighty-five, and it was the universal belief that every boy who read the Koran or studied the traditions in his presence, would assuredly attain to honour and happiness. For this cause did my father send me from Tús to Naishápur with Abd-u-samad, the doctor of law, that I might employ myself in study and learning under the guidance of that illustrious teacher. Towards me he ever turned an eye of favour and kindness, and as his pupil I felt for him extreme affection and devotion, so that I passed four years in his service. When I first came there, I found two other pupils of mine own age newly arrived, Hakim Omar Khayyám, and the ill-fated Ben Sabbáh. Both were endowed with sharpness of wit and the highest natural powers; and we three formed a close friendship together. When the Imám rose from his lectures, they used to join me, and we repeated to each other the lessons we had heard. Now Omar was a native of Naishápur, while Hasan Ben Sabbáh's father was one Ali, a man of austere life and practice, but heretical in his creed and doctrine. One day Hasan said to me and to Khayyám, 'It is a universal belief that the pupils of the Imám Mowaffak will attain to fortune. Now, even if we *all* do not attain thereto, without doubt one of us will; what then shall be our mutual pledge and bond?' We answered 'Be it what you please.' 'Well,' he said, 'let us make a vow, that to whomsoever this fortune falls, he shall share it equally with the rest, and reserve no pre-eminence for himself.' 'Be it so,' we both replied, and on these terms we mutually pledged our words. Years rolled on, and I went from Khorassan to Transoxiana, and wandered to Ghazni and Cabul; and when I returned, I was invested with office, and rose to be administrator of affairs during the Sultanate of Sultan Alp Arslán."

'He goes on to state, that years passed by, and both his old school-friends found him out, and came and claimed a share in his good fortune, according to the school-day vow. The Vizier was generous and kept his word. Hasan demanded a place in the government, which the Sultan granted at the Vizier's request; but discontented with a gradual rise, he plunged into the maze of intrigue of an oriental court, and, failing in a base attempt to supplant his benefactor, he was disgraced and fell. After many mishaps and wanderings, Hasan became the head of the Persian sect of the *Ismailians,*—a party of fanatics who had long murmured in obscurity, but rose to an evil eminence under the guidance of his strong and evil will. In A.D. 1090, he seized the castle of Alamút, in the province of Rúdbar, which lies in the mountainous tract, south of the Caspian Sea; and it was from this mountain home he obtained that evil celebrity among the Crusaders as the OLD MAN OF THE MOUNTAINS, and spread terror through the Mohammedan world; and it is yet disputed whether the word *Assassin*, which they have left in the language of modern Europe as their dark memorial, is derived from the *hashish*, or opiate of hemp-leaves (the

Indian *bhang*,) with which they maddened themselves to the sullen pitch of oriental desperation, or from the name of the founder of the dynasty, whom we have seen in his quiet collegiate days, at Naishápur. One of the countless victims of the Assassin's dagger was Nizám-ul-Mulk himself, the old school-boy friend.

'Omar Khayyám also came to the Vizier to claim his share; but not to ask for title or office. "The greatest boon you can confer on me," he said, "is to let me live in a corner under the shadow of your fortune, to spread wide the advantages of Science, and pray for your long life and prosperity." The Vizier tells us, that, when he found Omar was really sincere in his refusal, he pressed him no further, but granted him a yearly pension of 1200 *mithkáls* of gold, from the treasury of Naishápur.

'At Naishápur thus lived and died Omar Khayyám, "busied," adds the Vizier, "in winning knowledge of every kind, and especially in Astronomy, wherein he attained to a very high pre-eminence. Under the Sultanate of Malik Shah, he came to Merv, and obtained great praise for his proficiency in science, and the Sultan showered favours upon him."

'When Malik Shah determined to reform the calendar, Omar was one of the eight learned men employed to do it; the result was the *Jaláli* era (so called from *Jalal-ul-din*, one of the king's names,)—"a computation of time," says Gibbon, "which surpasses the Julian, and approaches the accuracy of the Gregorian style." He is also the author of some astronomical tables, entitled Ziji-

Maliksháhí,' and the French have lately republished and translated an Arabic Treatise of his on Algebra.

'These severer Studies, and his Verses, which, though happily fewer than any Persian Poet's, and, though perhaps fugitively composed, the Result of no fugitive Emotion or Thought, are probably the Work and Event of his Life, leaving little else to record. Perhaps he liked a little Farming too, so often as he speaks of the 'Edge of the Tilth' on which he loved to rest with his Diwán of Verse, his Loaf—and his Wine.

'His Takhallus or poetical name (Khayyám) signifies a Tent-maker, and he is said to have at one time exercised that trade, perhaps before Nizám-ul-Mulk's generosity raised him to independence. Many Persian poets similarly derive their names from their occupations; thus we have Attár, "a druggist," Assar, "an oil presser," &c.' (Though all these, like our Smiths, Archers, Millers, Fletchers, &c. may simply retain the Sirname of an hereditary calling.) 'Omar himself alludes to his name in the following whimsical lines:—

> "Khayyám, who stitched the tents of science,
> Has fallen in grief's furnace and been suddenly burned;
> The shears of Fate have cut the tent ropes of his life,
> And the broker of Hope has sold him for nothing!"

'We have only one more anecdote to give of his Life, and that relates to the close; related in the anonymous preface which is sometimes prefixed to his poems; it has been printed in the Persian in the Appendix to Hyde's

Veterum Persarum Religio, p. 499; and D'Herbelot alludes to it in his Bibliothèque, under *Khiam*:—*

"'It is written in the chronicles of the ancients that this King of the Wise, Omar Khayyám, died at Naishápur in the year of the Hegira, 517 (A.D. 1123); in science he was unrivalled—the very paragon of his age. Khwájah Nizámi of Samarcand, who was one of his pupils, relates the following story: 'I often used to hold conversations with my teacher, Omar Khayyám, in a garden; and one day he said to me, "my tomb shall be in a spot, where the north wind may scatter roses over it." I wondered at the words he spake, but I knew that his were no idle words. Years after, when I chanced to revisit Naishápur, I went to his final resting place, and lo! it was just outside a garden, and trees laden with fruit stretched their boughs over the garden wall, and dropped their flowers upon his tomb, so as the stone was hidden under them.'"

---

* Though *he* attributes the story to a Khiam, 'Philosophe Musulman qui a vécu en Odeur de Sainteté dans la Fin du premier et le Commencement du second Siècle,' ['Muslim philosopher who lived in "Odour of Sanctity", towards the end of the first and the beginning of the second centuries.'] no part of which, except the 'Philosophe,' can apply to *our* Khayyám, who, however, may claim the Story as *his*, on the Score of Rubáiyát, 67 and 68 of the present Version. The Rashness of the Words, according to D'Herbelot, consisted in being so opposed to those in the Koran: 'No Man knows where he shall die.'

Thus far—without fear of Trespass—from the Calcutta Review.

Though the Sultan 'shower'd Favours upon him,' Omar's Epicurean Audacity of Thought and Speech caused him to be regarded askance in his own Time and Country. He is said to have been especially hated and dreaded by the Súfis, whose Practice he ridiculed, and whose Faith amounts to little more than his own when stript of the Mysticism and formal Compliment to Islamism which Omar would not hide under. Their Poets, including Háfiz, who are (with the exception of Firdúsi) the most considerable in Persia, borrowed largely, indeed, of Omar's material, but turning it to a mystical Use more convenient to Themselves and the People they address'd; a People quite as quick of Doubt as of Belief; quite as keen of the Bodily Senses as of the Intellectual; and delighting in a cloudy Element compounded of all, in which they could float luxuriously between Heaven and Earth, and this World and the Next, on the wings of a poetical expression, that could be recited indifferently whether at the Mosque or the Tavern. Omar was too honest of Heart as well as of Head for this. Having failed (however mistakenly) of finding any Providence but Destiny, and any World but This, he set about making the most of it; preferring rather to soothe the Soul through the Senses into Acquiescence with Things as they were, than to perplex it with vain mortifications after what they *might be*. It has been seen that his Worldly Desires, however, were not exorbitant; and he very likely takes a humorous pleasure in exaggerating them above that Intellect in whose exercise he must have found great pleasure, though not in a Theological direction. However this may be, his Worldly Pleasures are what they profess to be without any Pretence at divine Allegory: his Wine is the veritable Juice of the Grape: his Tavern, where it was to be had: his Sáki, the Flesh and Blood that poured it out for him: all which, and where the Roses were in Bloom, was all he profess'd to want of this World or to expect of Paradise.

The Mathematic Faculty, too, which regulated his Fansy, and condensed his Verse to a Quality and Quantity unknown in Persian, perhaps in Oriental, Poetry, help'd by its very virtue perhaps to render him less popular with his countrymen. If the Greeks were Children in Gossip, what does Persian Literature imply but a *Second Childishness* of Garrulity? And certainly if no *ungeometric* Greek was to enter Plato's School of Philosophy, no so unchastised a Persian should enter on the Race of Persian Verse, with its 'fatal Facility' of running on long after Thought is winded! But Omar was not only the single Mathematician of his Country's Poets; he was also of that older Time and stouter Temper, before the native Soul of Persia was quite broke by a foreign Creed as well as foreign Conquest. Like his great Predecessor Firdúsi, who was as little of a *Mystic*; who scorned to use even a *Word* of the very language in which the New Faith came clothed; and who was suspected, not of Omar's Irreligion indeed, but of secretly clinging to the ancient Fire-Religion of Zerdusht, of which so many of the Kings he sang were Worshippers.

For whatever Reason, however, Omar, as before said, has never been popular in his own Country, and therefore has been but charily transmitted abroad. The MSS. of his Poems, mutilated beyond the average Casualties of Oriental Transcription, are so rare in the East as scarce to have reacht Westward at all, in spite of all that Arms and Science have brought us. There is none at the India House, none at the Bibliothèque Impériale of Paris. We know but of one in England: No. 140 of the Ouseley MSS. at the Bodleian, written at Shiraz, A.D. 1460. This contains but 158 Rubáiyát. One in the Asiatic Society's Library of Calcutta (of which we have a Copy) contains (and yet incomplete) 516, though swelled to that by all kinds of Repetition and Corruption. So Von Hammer speaks of *his* Copy as containing about 200, while Dr. Sprenger catalogues the Lucknow MS. at double that Number. The Scribes, too, of the Oxford and Calcutta MSS. seem to do their Work under a sort of Protest; each beginning with a Tetrastich (whether genuine or not) taken out of its alphabetical order; the Oxford with one of Apology; the Calcutta with one of Execration too stupid for Omar's, even had Omar been stupid enough to execrate himself.*

---

* 'Since this paper was written' (adds the Reviewer in a note) 'we have met with a Copy of a very rare Edition, printed at Calcutta in 1836. This contains 438 Tetrastichs, with an Appendix containing 54 others not found in some MSS.'

The Reviewer, who translates the foregoing Particulars of Omar's Life, and some of his Verse into Prose, concludes by comparing him with Lucretius, both in natural Temper and Genius, and as acted upon by the Circumstances in which he lived. Both indeed men of subtle Intellect and high Imagination, instructed in Learning beyond their day, and of Hearts passionate for Truth and Justice; who justly revolted from their Country's false Religion, and false, or foolish, Devotion to it; but who yet fell short of replacing what they subverted by any such better *Hope* as others, upon whom no better *Faith* had dawned, had yet made a Law to themselves. Lucretius, indeed, with such material as Epicurus furnished, consoled himself with the construction of a Machine that needed no Constructor, and acting by a Law that implied no Lawgiver; and so composing himself into a Stoical rather than Epicurean severity of Attitude, sat down to contemplate the mechanical Drama of the Universe of which he was part Actor; himself and all about him (as in his own sublime Description of the Roman Theatre,) coloured with the lurid reflex of the Curtain that was suspended between them and the outer Sun. Omar, more desperate, or more careless, of any such laborious System as resulted in nothing more than hopeless Necessity, flung his own Genius and Learning with a bitter jest into the general Ruin which their insufficient glimpses only served to reveal; and, yielding his Senses to the actual Rose and Vine, only *diverted* his thoughts by by balancing ideal possibilities of Fate, Freewill, Existence and Annihilation; with an oscillation that so generally inclined to the negative and lower side, as to make such Stanzas as the following exceptions to his general Philosophy—

> Oh, if my Soul can fling his Dust aside,
> And naked on the Air of Heaven ride,
>   Is't not a Shame, is't not a Shame for Him
> So long in this Clay Suburb to abide!

> Or is *that* but a Tent, where rests anon
> A Sultán to his Kingdom passing on,
>   And which the swarthy Chamberlain shall strike
> Then when the Sultán rises to be gone?

With regard to the present Translation. The original Rubáiyát (as, missing an Arabic Guttural, these *Tetrastichs* are more musically called), are independent Stanzas, consisting each of four Lines of equal, though varied, Prosody, sometimes *all* rhyming, but oftener (as here attempted) the third line suspending the Cadence by which the last atones with the former Two. Something as in the Greek Alcaic, where the third line seems to lift and suspend the Wave that falls over in the last. As usual with such kind of Oriental Verse, the Rubáiyát follow one another according to Alphabetic Rhyme—a strange Farrago of Grave and Gay. Those here selected are strung into something of an Eclogue, with perhaps a less than equal proportion of the 'Drink and make-merry,' which (genuine or not) recurs over-frequently in the Original. For Lucretian as Omar's Genius might be, he cross'd that darker Mood with much of Olivier de Basselin Humour. Any way, the Result is sad enough: saddest perhaps when most ostentatiously merry: any way, fitter to move Sorrow than Anger toward the old Tentmaker, who, after vainly endeavouring to unshackle his Steps from Destiny, and to catch some authentic Glimpse of TOMORROW, fell back upon TODAY (which has out-lasted so many Tomorrows!) as the only Ground he got to stand upon, however momentarily slipping from under his Feet.

RUBÁIYÁT

OF

OMAR KHAYYÁM OF NAISHÁPÚR

1

AWAKE ! for Morning in the Bowl of Night
Has flung the Stone that puts the Stars to Flight:[1]
    And Lo! the Hunter of the East has caught
The Sultán's Turret in a Noose of Light.

2

Dreaming when Dawn's Left Hand was in the Sky[2]
I heard a Voice within the Tavern cry,
    'Awake, my Little ones, and fill the Cup
Before Life's Liquor in its Cup be dry.'

3

And, as the Cock crew, those who stood before
The Tavern shouted—'Open then the Door!
    You know how little while we have to stay,
And, once departed, may return no more.'

4

Now the New Year[3] reviving old Desires,
The thoughtful Soul to Solitude retires,
　　Where the WHITE HAND OF MOSES on the Bough
Puts out,[4] and Jesus from the Ground suspires.

5

Irám indeed is gone with all its Rose,[5]
And Jamshýd's Sev'n-ring'd Cup where no one knows;
　　But still the Vine her ancient Ruby yields,
And still a Garden by the Water blows.

6

And David's Lips are lock't; but in divine
High-piping Péhlevi,[6] with 'Wine! Wine! Wine!
　　Red Wine!'—the Nightingale cries to the Rose
That yellow Cheek[7] of her's to'incarnadine.

7

Come, fill the Cup, and in the Fire of Spring
The Winter Garment of Repentance fling:
　　The Bird of Time has but a little way
To fly—and Lo! the Bird is on the Wing.

8

And look—a thousand Blossoms with the Day
Woke—and a thousand scatter'd into Clay:
　　And this first Summer Month that brings the Rose
Shall take Jamshýd and Kaikobád away.

9

But come with old Khayyám, and leave the Lot
Of Kaikobád and Kaikhosrú forgot:
    Let Rustum lay about him as he will,[8]
Or Hátim Tai cry Supper—heed them not.

10

With me along some Strip of Herbage strown
That just divides the desert from the sown,
    Where name of Slave and Sultán scarce is known,
And pity Sultán Máhmúd on his Throne.

11

Here with a Loaf of Bread beneath the Bough,
A Flask of Wine, a Book of Verse—and Thou
    Beside me singing in the Wilderness—
And Wilderness is Paradise enow.

12

'How sweet is mortal Sovranty!'—think some:
Others—'How blest the Paradise to come!'
    Ah, take the Cash in hand and waive the Rest;
Oh, the brave Music of a *distant* Drum![9]

13

Look to the Rose that blows about us—'Lo,
Laughing,' she says, 'into the World I blow:
    At once the silken Tassel of my Purse
Tear, and its Treasure[10] on the Garden throw.'

14

The Worldly Hope men set their Hearts upon
Turns Ashes—or it prospers; and anon,
    Like Snow upon the Desert's dusty Face
Lighting a little Hour or two—is gone.

15

And those who husbanded the Golden Grain,
And those who flung it to the Winds like Rain,
    Alike to no such aureate Earth are turn'd
As, buried once, Men want dug up again.

16

Think, in this batter'd Caravanserai
Whose Doorways are alternate Night and Day,
    How Sultán after Sultán with his Pomp
Abode his Hour or two, and went his way.

17

They say the Lion and the Lizard keep
The Courts where Jamshýd gloried and drank deep:[11]
    And Bahrám, that great Hunter—the Wild Ass
Stamps o'er his Head, and he lies fast asleep.

18

I sometimes think that never blows so red
The Rose as where some buried Cæsar bled;
    That every Hyacinth the Garden wears
Dropt in its Lap from some once lovely Head.

19

And this delightful Herb whose tender Green
Fledges the River's Lip on which we lean—
    Ah, lean upon it lightly! for who knows
From what once lovely Lip it springs unseen!

20

Ah, my Belovéd, fill the cup that clears
TO-DAY of past Regrets and future Fears—
    To-morrow?—Why, To-morrow I may be
Myself with Yesterday's Sev'n Thousand Years.[12]

21

Lo! some we loved, the loveliest and the best
That Time and Fate of all their Vintage prest,
    Have drunk their Cup a Round or two before,
And one by one crept silently to Rest.

22

And we, that now make merry in the Room
They left, and Summer dresses in new Bloom,
    Ourselves must we beneath the Couch of Earth
Descend, ourselves to make a Couch—for whom?

23

Ah, make the most of what we yet may spend,
Before we too into the Dust descend;
    Dust into Dust, and under Dust, to lie,
Sans Wine, sans Song, sans Singer, and—sans End!

24

Alike for those who for TO-DAY prepare,
And those that after a TO-MORROW stare,
    A Muezzín from the Tower of Darkness cries
'Fools! your Reward is neither Here nor There!'

25

Why, all the Saints and Sages who discuss'd
Of the Two Worlds so learnedly, are thrust
    Like foolish Prophets forth; their Words to Scorn
Are scatter'd, and their Mouths are stopt with Dust.

26

Oh, come with old Khayyám, and leave the Wise
To talk; one thing is certain, that Life flies;
    One thing is certain, and the Rest is Lies;
The Flower that once has blown for ever dies.

27

Myself when young did eagerly frequent
Doctor and Saint, and heard great Argument
    About it and about: but evermore
Came out by the same Door as in I went.

28

With them the Seed of Wisdom did I sow,
And with my own hand labour'd it to grow:
    And this was all the Harvest that I reap'd—
'I came like Water, and like Wind I go.'

29

Into this Universe, and *why* not knowing,
Nor *whence*, like Water willy-nilly flowing:
    And out of it, as Wind along the Waste,
I know not *whither*, willy-nilly blowing.

30

What, without asking, hither hurried *whence?*
And, without asking, *whither* hurried hence!
    Another and another Cup to drown
The Memory of this Impertinence!

31

Up from Earth's Centre through the Seventh Gate
I rose, and on the Throne of Saturn sate,[13]
    And many Knots unravel'd by the Road;
But not the Knot of Human Death and Fate.

32

There was a Door to which I found no Key:
There was a Veil past which I could not see:
    Some little Talk awhile of ME and THEE
There seemed—and then no more of THEE and ME.[14]

33

Then to the rolling Heav'n itself I cried,
Asking, 'What Lamp had Destiny to guide
    Her little Children stumbling in the Dark?'
And—'A blind Understanding!' Heav'n replied.

34

Then to the earthen Bowl did I adjourn
My Lip the secret Well of Life to learn:
    And Lip to Lip it murmur'd—'While you live
Drink!—for once dead you never shall return.'

35

I think the Vessel, that with fugitive
Articulation answer'd, once did live,
    And merry-make; and the cold Lip I kiss'd
How many kisses might it take—and give!

36

For in the Market-place, one Dusk of Day,
I watch'd the Potter thumping his wet Clay:
    And with its all obliterated Tongue
It murmur'd—'Gently, Brother, gently, pray!'

37

Ah, fill the Cup:—what boots it to repeat
How Time is slipping underneath our Feet:
    Unborn TO-MORROW, and dead YESTERDAY,
Why fret about them if TO-DAY be sweet!

38

One Moment in Annihilation's Waste,
One Moment, of the Well of Life to taste—
    The Stars are setting and the Caravan
Starts for the Dawn of Nothing[15]—Oh, make haste!

39
How long, how long, in infinite Pursuit
Of This and That endeavour and dispute?
    Better be merry with the fruitful Grape
Than sadden after none, or bitter, Fruit.

40
You know, my Friends, how long since in my House
For a new Marriage I did make Carouse:
    Divorced old barren Reason from my Bed,
And took the Daughter of the Vine to Spouse.

41
For 'Is' and 'Is-not' though *with* Rule and Line,
And 'Up-and-down' *without*, I could define,[16]
    I yet in all I only cared to know,
Was never deep in anything but—Wine.

42
And lately, by the Tavern Door agape,
Came stealing through the Dusk an Angel Shape
    Bearing a Vessel on his Shoulder; and
He bid me taste of it; and 'twas—the Grape!

43
The Grape that can with Logic absolute
The Two-and-Seventy jarring Sects[17] confute:
    The subtle Alchemist that in a Trice
Life's leaden Metal into Gold transmute.

44

The mighty Mahmúd, the victorious Lord,
That all the misbelieving and black Horde[18]
   Of Fears and Sorrows that infest the Soul
Scatters and slays with his enchanted Sword.

45

But leave the Wise to wrangle, and with me
The Quarrel of the Universe let be:
   And, in some corner of the Hubbub coucht,
Make Game of that which makes as much of Thee.

46

For in and out, above, about, below,
'Tis nothing but a Magic Shadow-show,
   Play'd in a Box whose Candle is the Sun,
Round which we Phantom Figures come and go.[19]

47

And if the Wine you drink, the Lip you press,
End in the Nothing all Things end in—Yes—
   Then fancy while Thou art, Thou art but what
Thou shalt be—Nothing—Thou shalt not be less.

48

While the Rose blows along the River Brink,
With old Khayyám the Ruby Vintage drink:
   And when the Angel with his darker Draught
Draws up to Thee—take that, and do not shrink.

49

'Tis all a Chequer-board of Nights and Days
Where Destiny with Men for Pieces plays:
    Hither and thither moves, and mates, and slays,
And one by one back in the Closet lays.

50

The Ball no Question makes of Ayes and Noes,
But Right or Left as strikes the Player goes;
    And He that toss'd Thee down into the Field,
He knows about it all—HE knows—HE knows![20]

51

The Moving Finger writes; and, having writ,
Moves on: nor all thy Piety nor Wit
    Shall lure it back to cancel half a Line,
Nor all thy Tears wash out a Word of it.

52

And that inverted Bowl we call The Sky,
Whereunder crawling coop't we live and die,
    Lift not thy hands to *It* for help—for It
Rolls impotently on as Thou or I.

53

With Earth's first Clay They did the Last Man knead,
And then of the Last Harvest sow'd the Seed:
    Yea, the first Morning of Creation wrote
What the Last Dawn of Reckoning shall read.

54

I tell Thee this—When, starting from the Goal,
Over the shoulders of the flaming Foal
    Of Heav'n Parwín and Mushtara they flung,[21]
In my predestin'd Plot of Dust and Soul

55

The Vine had struck a Fibre; which about
If clings my Being—let the Súfi flout;
    Of my Base Metal may be filed a Key,
That shall unlock the Door he howls without.

56

And this I know: whether the one True Light,
Kindle to Love, or Wrathconsume me quite,
    One Glimpse of It within the Tavern caught
Better than in the Temple lost outright.

57

Oh Thou, who didst with Pitfall and with Gin
Beset the Road I was to wander in,
    Thou wilt not with Predestination round
Enmesh me, and impute my Fall to Sin?

58

Oh, Thou, who Man of baser Earth didst make,
And who with Eden didst devise the Snake;
    For all the Sin wherewith the Face of Man
Is blacken'd, Man's Forgiveness give—and take!

✶ ✶ ✶ ✶ ✶ ✶ ✶ ✶

KÚZA – NÁMA

59
Listen again. One Evening at the Close
Of Ramazán, ere the better Moon arose,
   In that old Potter's Shop I stood alone
With the clay Population round in Rows.

60
And, strange to tell, among that Earthern Lot
Some could articulate, while others not:
   And suddenly one more impatient cried—
'Who *is* the Potter, pray, and who the Pot?'

61
Then said another—'Surely not in vain
My substance from the common Earth was ta'en,
   That He who subtly wrought me into Shape
Should stamp me back to common Earth again.'

62
Another said—'Why, ne'er a peevish Boy,
Would break the Bowl from which he drank in Joy;
   Shall He that *made* the Vessel in pure Love
And Fancy, in an after Rage destroy!'

63

None answer'd this; but after Silence spake
A Vessel of a more ungainly Make:
    'They sneer at me for leaning all awry;
What! did the Hand then of the Potter shake?'

64

Said one—'Folks of a surly Tapster tell,
And daub his Visage with the Smoke of Hell;
    They talk of some strict Testing of us—Pish!
He's a Good Fellow, and 'twill all be well.'

65

Then said another with a long-drawn Sigh,
'My Clay with long oblivion is gone dry:
    But, fill me with the old familiar Juice,
Methinks I might recover by-and-bye.'

66

So while the Vessels one by one were speaking,
One spied the little Crescent all were seeking:[22]
    And then they jogg'd each other, 'Brother! Brother!
Hark to the Porter's Shoulder-knot a-creaking!'

✳ ✳ ✳ ✳ ✳ ✳ ✳ ✳

67

Ah, with the Grape my fading Life provide,
And wash my Body whence the Life has died,
    And in a Windingsheet of Vine-leaf wrapt,
So bury me by some sweet Garden-side.

68

That ev'n my buried Ashes such a Snare
Of Perfume shall fling up into the Air,
    As not a True Believer passing by
But shall be overtaken unaware.

69

Indeed the Idols I have loved so long
Have done my Credit in Men's Eye much wrong:
    Have drown'd my Honour in a shallow Cup,
And sold my Reputation for a Song.

70

Indeed, indeed, Repentance oft before
I swore—but was I sober when I swore?
    And then and then came Spring, and Rose-in-hand
My thread-bare Penitence apieces tore.

71

And much as Wine has play'd the Infidel,
And robb'd me of my Robe of Honour—well,
    I often wonder what the Vintners buy
One half so precious as the Goods they sell.

72

Alas, that Spring should vanish with the Rose!
That Youth's sweet-scented Manuscript should close!
    The Nightingale that in the Branches sang,
Ah, whence, and whither flown again, who knows!

73

Ah Love! could thou and I with Fate conspire
To grasp this sorry Scheme of Things entire,
    Would not we shatter it to bits—and then
Re-mould it nearer to the Heart's Desire!

74

Ah, Moon of my Delight who know'st no wane,
The Moon of Heav'n is rising once again:
    How oft hereafter rising shall she look
Through this same Garden after me—in vain!

75

And when Thyself with shining Foot shall pass
Among the Guests Star-scatter'd on the Grass,
    And in thy joyous Errand reach the Spot
Where I made one—turn down an empty Glass!

TAMÁM SHUD

NOTES*

[1] Flinging a Stone into the Cup was the Signal for 'To Horse!' in the Desert.

[2] The *'False Dawn;' Subhi Kházib*, a transient Light on the Horizon about an hour before the *Subhi sâdhik*, or True Dawn; a well known Phenomenon in the East. The Persians call the Morning Gray, or Dusk, *'Wolf-and-Sheep-While.'* 'Almost at odds with, which is which.'

[3] New Year. Beginning with the Vernal Equinox, it must be remembered; and (howsoever the old Solar Year is practically superseded by the clumsy *Lunar* Year that dates from the Mohammedan Hijra) still commemorated by a Festival that is said to have been appointed by the very Jamshyd whom Omar so often talks of, and whose yearly Calendar he helped to rectify.

'The sudden approach and rapid advance of the Spring,' (says a late Traveller in Persia) 'are very striking. Before the Snow is well off the Ground, the Trees burst into Blossom, and the Flowers start from the Soil. At *Now Rooz* (*their* New Year's Day) the Snow was lying

---

* [The first edition of the *Rubáiyát* indicated the presence of notes by superscript numerals appearing in the stanzas.—KS]

in patches on the Hills and in the shaded Vallies, while the Fruit-trees in the Garden were budding beautifully, and green Plants and Flowers springing upon the Plains on every side—

> And on old Hyem's Chin and icy Crown
> An odorous Chaplet of sweet Summer buds
> Is, as in mockery, set— —

Among the Plants newly appear'd I recognized some old Acquaintances I had not seen for many a Year: among these, two varieties of the Thistle; a coarse species of the Daisy, like the Horse-gowan; red and white Clover; the Dock; the blue Corn-flower; and that vulgar Herb the Dandelion rearing its yellow crest on the Banks of the Watercourses.' The Nightingale was not yet heard, for the Rose was not yet blown: but an almost identical Blackbird and Woodpecker helped to make up something of a North-country Spring.

⁴ Exodus iv. 6; where Moses draws forth his Hand—not, according to the Persians, *'leprous as Snow,'*—but *white* as our May-Blossom in Spring perhaps! According to them also the Healing Power of Jesus resided in his Breath.

⁵ Irám, planted by King Schedad, and now sunk somewhere in the Sands of Arabia. Jamshyd's Seven-ring'd Cup was typical of the Seven Heavens, 7 Planets, 7 Seas, &c. and was a *Divining Cup*.

NOTES TO THE FIRST EDITION

[6] *Péhlevi*, the old Heroic *Sanskrit* of Persia. Háfiz also speaks of the Nightingale's *Péhlevi*, which did not change with the People's.

[7] I am not sure if this refers to the Red Rose looking sickly, or the Yellow Rose that ought to be Red; Red, White, and Yellow Roses all common in Persia.

[8] Rustum, the 'Hercules' of Persia, whose exploits are among the most celebrated in the Shah-náma. Hátim Tai, a well-known Type of Oriental Generosity.

[9] A Drum—beaten outside a Palace.

[10] That is, the Rose's Golden Centre.

[11] Persepolis: call'd also *Takht'i Jamshyd*—THE THRONE OF JAMSHYD, '*King Splendid*,' of the mythical *Peeshdádian* Dynasty, and supposed (with Shah-náma Authority) to have been founded and built by him, though others refer it to the Work of the Genie King, Ján Ibn Jann, who also built the Pyramids before the time of Adam. It is also called *Chehl-minar—Forty-column*; which is Persian, probably, for *Column-countless*; the Hall they adorned or supported with their Lotus Base and taurine Capital indicating double that Number, though now counted down to less than half by Earthquake and other Inroad. By whomsoever built, unquestionably the Monument of a long extinguished Dynasty and Mythology; its Halls, Chambers and Galleries, inscribed with Arrow-head Characters, and sculptured with colossal, wing'd, half human Figures like those of Nimrod; Processions of Priests and Warriors—(doubtful if any where a Woman)—and Kings sitting on Thrones or in Chariots,

Staff of Lotus-flower in hand, and the *Ferooher*—Symbol of Existence—with his wing'd Globe, common also to Assyria and Ægypt—over their heads. All this, together with Aqueduct and Cistern, and other Appurtenance of a Royal Palace, upon a Terrace-platform, ascended by a double Flight of Stairs that may be gallop'd up, and cut out of and into the Rock-side of the *Koh'i Ráhmet, Mountain of Mercy*, where the old Fire-worshiping Sovereigns are buried, and overlooking the Plain of Merdasht.

Persians, like some other People, it seems, love to write their own Names, with sometimes a Verse or two, on their Country's Monuments. Mr. Binning (from whose sensible Travels the foregoing Account is mainly condens't) found several such in Persepolis; in one Place a fine Line of Háfiz: in another 'an original, no doubt,' he says, 'by no great Poet,' however 'right in his Sentiment.' The Words somehow looked to us, and the 'halting metre' sounded, familiar; and on looking back at last among the 500 Rubáyiát of the Calcutta Omar MS.—*there* it is: old Omar quoted by *one* of his Countrymen, and here turned into hasty Rhyme, at any rate—

> This Palace that its Top to Heaven threw,
> And Kings their Forehead on its Threshold drew—
>   I saw a Ring-dove sitting there alone,
> And 'Coo, Coo, Coo,' she cried, and 'Coo, Coo, Coo.'

So it seems the Persian speaks the English Ring-dove's *Péhlevi*, which is also articulate Persian for 'Where?'

BAHRÁM GÚR—*Bahrám of the Wild Ass*, from his Fame in hunting it—a Sassanian Sovereign, had also his Seven Castles (like the King of Bohemia!) each of a different Colour; each with a Royal Mistress within side; each of whom recounts to Bahrám a Romance, according to one of the most famous Poems of Persia, written by Amír Khusraw: these Sevens also figuring (according to Eastern Mysticism) the Seven Heavens, and perhaps the Book itself that Eighth, into which the mystical Seven transcend, and within which they revolve. The Ruins of Three of these Towers are yet shown by the Peasantry; as also the Swamp in which Bahrám sunk, like the Master of Ravenswood, while pursuing his *Gúr*.

[12] A thousand years to each Planet.

[13] Saturn, Lord of the Seventh Heaven.

[14] ME-AND-THEE; that is, some Dividual Existence or Personality apart from the Whole.

[15] The Caravan travelling by Night (after their New Year's Day of the Vernal Equinox) by command of Mohammed, I believe.

[16] A Laugh at his Mathematics perhaps.

[17] The 72 Sects into which Islamism so soon split.

[18] This alludes to Mahmúd's Conquest of India and its swarthy Idolaters.

[19] *Fanúsi khiyál*, a Magic-lanthorn still used in India; the cylindrical Interior being painted with various Figures, and so lightly poised and ventilated as to revolve round the Candle lighted within.

[20] A very mysterious Line in the Original;

U dánad u dánad u dánad u ——

breaking off something like our Wood-pigeon's Note, which she is said to take up just where she left off.

[21] Parwín and Mushtara—The Pleiads and Jupiter.

[22] At the Close of the Fasting Month, Ramazán (which makes the Musulman unhealthy and unamiable), the first Glimpse of the New Moon (who rules their Division of the Year) is looked for with the utmost Anxiety, and hailed with all Acclamation. Then it is that the Porter's Knot may be heard toward the *Cellar*, perhaps. Old Omar has elsewhere a pretty Quatrain about this same Moon—

> Be of Good Cheer—the sullen Month will die,
> And a young Moon requite us by and bye:
>   Look how the Old one meagre, bent, and wan
> With Age and Fast, is fainting from the Sky!

FINIS

RUBÁIYÁT
OF
OMAR KHAYYÁM

SECOND EDITION

1868

RUBÁIYÁT

OF

OMAR KHAYYÁM OF NAISHÁPÚR

1

WAKE ! For the Sun behind yon Eastern height
Has chased the Session of the Stars from Night;
    And, to the field of Heav'n ascending, strikes
The Sultán's Turret with a Shaft of Light.

2

Before the phantom of False morning died,
Methought a Voice within the Tavern cried,
    'When all the Temple is prepared within,
Why lags the drowsy Worshipper outside?'

3

And, as the Cock crew, those who stood before
The Tavern shouted—'Open then the Door!
    You know how little while we have to stay,
And, once departed, may return no more.'

4

Now the New Year reviving old Desires,
The thoughtful Soul to Solitude retires,
　　Where the WHITE HAND OF MOSES on the Bough
Puts out, and Jesus from the Ground suspires.

5

Iram indeed is gone with all his Rose,
And Jamshýd's Sev'n-ring'd Cup where no one knows;
　　But still a Ruby gushes from the Vine,
And many a Garden by the Water blows.

6

And David's lips are lockt; but in divine
High-piping Péhlevi, with 'Wine! Wine! Wine!
　　Red Wine!'—the Nightingale cries to the Rose
That sallow cheek of her's to incarnadine.

7

Come, fill the Cup, and in the fire of Spring
Your Winter-garment of Repentance fling:
　　The Bird of Time has but a little way
To flutter—and the Bird is on the Wing.

8

Whether at Naishápúr or Babylon,
Whether the Cup with sweet or bitter run,
　　The Wine of Life keeps oozing drop by drop,
The Leaves of Life keep falling one by one.

9

Morning a thousand Roses brings, you say;
Yes, but where leaves the Rose of yesterday?
    And this first Summer month that brings the Rose
Shall take Jamshýd and Kaikobád away.

10

Well, let it take them! What have we to do
With Kaikobád the Great, or Kaikhosrú?
    Let Rustum cry 'To Battle!' as he likes,
Or Hátim Tai 'To Supper!'—heed not you.

11

With me along the strip of Herbage strown
That just divides the desert from the sown,
    Where name of Slave and Sultán is forgot—
And Peace to Máhmúd on his golden Throne!

12

Here with a little Bread beneath the Bough,
A Flask of Wine, a Book of Verse—and Thou
    Beside me singing in the Wilderness—
Oh, Wilderness were Paradise enow!

13

Some for the Glories of This World; and some
Sigh for the Prophet's Paradise to come;
    Ah, take the Cash, and let the Promise go,
Nor heed the music of a distant Drum!

14

Were it not Folly, Spider-like to spin
The Thread of present Life away to win—
  What? for ourselves, who know not if we shall
Breathe out the very Breath we now breathe in!

15

Look to the blowing Rose about us—'Lo,
Laughing,' she says, 'into the world I blow:
  At once the silken tassel of my Purse
Tear, and its Treasure on the Garden throw.'

16

For those who husbanded the Golden grain,
And those who flung it to the winds like Rain,
  Alike to no such aureate Earth are turn'd
As, buried once, Men want dug up again.

17

The Worldly Hope men set their Hearts upon
Turns Ashes—or it prospers; and anon,
  Like Snow upon the Desert's dusty Face,
Lighting a little hour or two—was gone.

18

Think, in this batter'd Caravanserai
Whose Portals are alternate Night and Day,
  How Sultán after Sultán with his Pomp
Abode his destin'd Hour, and went his way.

19

They say the Lion and the Lizard keep
The Courts where Jamshýd gloried and drank deep:
    And Bahrám, that great Hunter—the Wild Ass
Stamps o'er his Head, but cannot break his Sleep.

20

The Palace that to Heav'n his pillars threw,
And Kings the forehead on his threshold drew—
    I saw the solitary Ringdove there,
And 'Coo, coo, coo,' she cried; and 'Coo, coo, coo.'

21

Ah, my Belovéd, fill the Cup that clears
TO-DAY of past Regrets and future Fears:
    To-morrow!—Why, To-morrow I may he
Myself with Yesterday's Sev'n thousand Years.

22

For some we loved, the loveliest and the best
That from his Vintage rolling Time has prest,
    Have drunk their Cup a Round or two before,
And one by one crept silently to rest.

23

And we, that now make merry in the Room
They left, and Summer dresses in new Bloom,
    Ourselves must we beneath the Couch of Earth
Descend, ourselves to make a Couch—for whom?

24

I sometimes think that never blows so red
The Rose as where some buried Cæsar bled;
    That every Hyacinth the Garden wears
Dropt in her Lap from some once lovely Head.

25

And this delightful Herb whose living Green
Fledges the River's Lip on which we lean—
    Ah, lean upon it lightly! for who knows
From what once lovely Lip it springs unseen!

26

Ah, make the most of what we yet may spend,
Before we too into the Dust descend;
    Dust into Dust, and under Dust, to lie,
Sans Wine, sans Song, sans Singer, and—sans End!

27

Alike for those who for TO-DAY prepare,
And those that after some TO-MORROW stare,
    A Muezzín from the Tower of Darkness cries,
'Fools! your Reward is neither Here nor There!'

28

Another Voice, when I am sleeping, cries,
'The Flower should open with the Morning skies.'
    And a retreating Whisper, as I wake—
'The Flower that once has blown for ever dies.'

29

Why, all the Saints and Sages who discuss'd
Of the Two Worlds so learnedly, are thrust
   Like foolish Prophets forth; their Words to Scorn
Are scatter'd, and their Mouths are stopt with Dust.

30

Myself when young did eagerly frequent
Doctor and Saint, and heard great argument
   About it and about: but evermore
Came out by the same door as in I went.

31

With them the seed of Wisdom did I sow,
And with my own hand wrought to make it grow:
   And this was all the Harvest that I reap'd—
'I came like Water, and like Wind I go.'

32

Into this Universe, and *Why* not knowing,
Nor *Whence*, like Water willy-nilly flowing:
   And out of it, as Wind along the Waste,
I know not *Whither*, willy-nilly blowing.

33

What, without asking, hither hurried *Whence?*
And, without asking, *Whither* hurried hence!
   Ah, contrite Heav'n endowed us with the Vine
To drug the memory of that insolence!

34

Up from Earth's Centre through the Seventh Gate
I rose, and on the Throne of Saturn sate,
   And many Knots unravel'd by the Road;
But not the Master-Knot of Human Fate.

35

There was the Door to which I found no Key:
There was the Veil through which I could not see:
   Some little talk awhile of ME and THEE
There was—and then no more of THEE and ME.

36

Earth could not answer: nor the Seas that mourn
In flowing Purple, of their Lord forlorn;
   Nor Heav'n, with those eternal Signs reveal'd
And hidden by the sleeve of Night and Morn.

37

Then of the THEE IN ME who works behind
The Veil of Universe I cried to find
   A Lamp to guide me through the darkness; and
Something then said—'An Understanding blind.'

38

Then to the Lip of this poor earthen Urn
I lean'd, the secret Well of Life to learn:
   And Lip to Lip it murmur'd—'While you live,
'Drink!—for, once dead, you never shall return.'

39

I think the Vessel, that with fugitive
Articulation answer'd, once did live,
    And drink; and that impassive Lip I kiss'd,
How many Kisses might it take—and give!

40

For I remember stopping by the way
To watch a Potter thumping his wet Clay:
    And with its all-obliterated Tongue
It murmur'd—'Gently, Brother, gently, pray!'

41

For has not such a Story from of Old
Down Man's successive generations roll'd
    Of such a clod of saturated Earth
Cast by the Maker into Human mould?

42

And not a drop that from our Cups we throw
On the parcht herbage but may steal below
    To quench the fire of Anguish in some Eye
There hidden—far beneath, and long ago.

43

As then the Tulip for her wonted sup
Of Heavenly Vintage lifts her chalice up,
    Do you, twin offspring of the soil, till Heav'n
To Earth invert you like an empty Cup.

44

Do you, within your little hour of Grace,
The waving Cypress in your Arms enlace,
  Before the Mother back into her arms
Fold, and dissolve you in a last embrace.

45

And if the Cup you drink, the Lip you press,
End in what All begins and ends in—Yes;
  Imagine then you *are* what heretofore
You *were*—hereafter you shall not be less.

46

So when at last the Angel of the drink
Of Darkness finds you by the river-brink,
  And, proffering his Cup, invites your Soul
Forth to your Lips to quaff it—do not shrink.

47

And fear not lest Existence closing *your*
Account, should lose, or know the type no more;
  The Eternal Sáki from that Bowl has pour'd
Millions of Bubbles like us, and will pour.

48

When You and I behind the Veil are past,
Oh but the long long while the World shall last,
  Which of our Coming and Departure heeds
As much as Ocean of a pebble-cast.

49

One Moment in Annihilation's Waste,
One Moment, of the Well of Life to taste—
　　The Stars are setting, and the Caravan
Draws to the Dawn of Nothing—Oh make haste!

50

Would you that spangle of Existence spend
About THE SECRET—quick about it, Friend!
　　A Hair, they say, divides the False and True—
And upon what, prithee, does Life depend?

51

A Hair, they say, divides the False and True;
Yes; and a single Alif were the clue,
　　Could you but find it, to the Treasure-house,
And peradventure to THE MASTER too;

52

Whose secret Presence, through Creation's veins
Running, Quicksilver-like eludes your pains:
　　Taking all shapes from Máh to Máhi; and
They change and perish all—but He remains;

53

A moment guess'd—then back behind the Fold
Immerst of Darkness round the Drama roll'd
　　Which, for the Pastime of Eternity,
He does Himself contrive, enact, behold.

54

But if in vain, down on the stubborn floor
Of Earth, and up to Heav'n's unopening Door,
    You gaze To-day, while You are You—how then
To-morrow, You when shall be You no more?

55

Oh, plagued no more with Human or Divine,
To-morrow's tangle to itself resign,
    And lose your fingers in the tresses of
The Cypress-slender Minister of Wine.

56

Waste not your Hour, nor in the vain pursuit
Of This and That endeavour and dispute;
    Better be merry with the fruitful Grape
Than sadden after none, or bitter, Fruit.

57

You know, my Friends, how bravely in my House
For a new Marriage I did make Carouse:
    Divorced old barren Reason from my Bed,
And took the Daughter of the Vine to Spouse.

58

For 'Is' and 'Is-not' though with Rule and Line,
And 'Up-and-down' by Logic I define,
    Of all that one should care to fathom, I
Was never deep in anything but—Wine.

59

Ah, but my Computations, People say,
Have squared the Year to human compass, eh?
    If so, by striking from the Calendar
Unborn To-morrow, and dead Yesterday.

60

And lately, by the Tavern Door agape,
Came shining through the Dusk an Angel Shape
    Bearing a Vessel on his Shoulder; and
He bid me taste of it; and 'twas—the Grape!

61

The Grape that can with Logic absolute
The Two-and-Seventy jarring Sects confute:
    The sovereign Alchemist that in a trice
Life's leaden metal into Gold transmute:

62

The mighty Mahmúd, Allah-breathing Lord,
That all the misbelieving and black Horde
    Of Fears and Sorrows that infest the Soul
Scatters before him with his whirlwind Sword.

63

Why, be this Juice the growth of God, who dare
Blaspheme the twisted tendril as a Snare?
    A Blessing, we should use it, should we not?
And if a Curse—why, then, Who set it there?

64

I must abjure the Balm of Life, I must,
Scared by some After-reckoning ta'en on trust,
  Or lured with Hope of some Diviner Drink,
When the frail Cup is crumbled into Dust!

65

If but the Vine and Love-abjuring Band
Are in the Prophet's Paradise to stand,
  Alack, I doubt the Prophet's Paradise
Were empty as the hollow of one's Hand.

66

Oh threats of Hell and Hopes of Paradise!
One thing at least is certain—*This* Life flies:
  One thing is certain and the rest is Lies;
The Flower that once is blown for ever dies.

67

Strange, is it not? that of the myriads who
Before us pass'd the door of Darkness through
  Not one returns to tell us of the Road,
Which to discover we must travel too.

68

The Revelations of Devout and Learn'd
Who rose before us, and as Prophets burn'd,
  Are all but Stories, which, awoke from Sleep
They told their fellows, and to Sleep return'd.

69

Why, if the Soul can fling the Dust aside,
And naked on the Air of Heaven ride,
    Is't not a shame—is't not a shame for him
So long in this Clay suburb to abide!

70

But that is but a Tent wherein may rest
A Sultan to the realm of Death addrest;
    The Sultan rises, and the dark Ferrásh
Strikes, and prepares it for another guest.

71

I sent my Soul through the Invisible,
Some letter of that After-life to spell:
    And after many days my Soul return'd
And said, 'Behold, Myself am Heav'n and Hell :'

72

Heav'n but the Vision of fulfill'd Desire,
And Hell the Shadow of a Soul on fire,
    Cast on the Darkness into which Ourselves,
So late emerg'd from, shall so soon expire.

73

We are no other than a moving row
Of visionary Shapes that come and go
    Round with this Sun-illumin'd Lantern held
In Midnight by the Master of the Show;

74

Impotent Pieces of the Game He plays
Upon this Chequer-board of Nights and Days;
    Hither and thither moves, and checks, and slays;
And one by one back in the Closet lays.

75

The Ball no Question makes of Ayes and Noes,
But Right or Left as strikes the Player goes;
    And He that toss'd you down into the Field,
He knows about it all—HE knows—HE knows!

76

The Moving Finger writes; and, having writ,
Moves on: nor all your Piety nor Wit
    Shall lure it back to cancel half a Line,
Nor all your Tears wash out a Word of it.

77

For let Philosopher and Doctor preach
Of what they will, and what they will not—each
    Is but one Link in an eternal Chain
That none can slip, nor break, nor over-reach.

78

And that inverted Bowl we call The Sky,
Whereunder crawling coop'd we live and die,
    Lift not your hands to *It* for help—for It
As impotently rolls as you or I.

79

With Earth's first Clay They did the Last Man knead,
And there of the Last Harvest sow'd the Seed:
   And the first Morning of Creation wrote
What the Last Dawn of Reckoning shall read.

80

Yesterday *This* Day's Madness did prepare:
To-morrow's Silence, Triumph, or Despair:
   Drink! for you know not whence you came, nor why:
Drink! for you know not why you go, nor where.

81

I tell you this—When, started from the Goal,
Over the flaming shoulders of the Foal
   Of Heav'n Parwín and Mushtari they flung,
In my predestin'd Plot of Dust and Soul

82

The Vine had struck a fibre: which about
If clings my Being—let the Dervish flout;
   Of my Base metal may be filed a Key,
That shall unlock the Door he howls without.

83

And this I know: whether the one True Light,
Kindle to Love, or Wrath-consume me quite,
   One Flash of It within the Tavern caught
Better than in the Temple lost outright.

84

What! out of senseless Nothing to provoke
A conscious Something to resent the yoke
    Of unpermitted Pleasure, under pain
Of Everlasting Penalties, if broke!

85

What! from his helpless Creature be repaid
Pure Gold for what he lent us dross-allay'd—
    Sue for a Debt we never did contract,
And cannot answer—Oh the sorry trade!

86

Nay, but, for terror of his wrathful Face,
I swear I will not call Injustice Grace;
    Not one Good Fellow of the Tavern but
Would kick so poor a Coward from the place.

87

Oh Thou, who didst with pitfall and with gin
Beset the Road I was to wander in,
    Thou wilt not with Predestin'd Evil round
Enmesh, and then impute my Fall to Sin?

88

Oh Thou, who Man of baser Earth didst make,
And ev'n with Paradise devise the Snake:
    For all the Sin the Face of wretched Man
Is black with—Man's Forgiveness give—and take!

✻ ✻ ✻ ✻ ✻ ✻ ✻ ✻

89

As under cover of departing Day
Slunk hunger-stricken Ramazán away,
  Once more within the Potter's house alone
I stood, surrounded by the Shapes of Clay.

90

And once again there gather'd a scarce heard
Whisper among them; as it were, the stirr'd
  Ashes of some all but extinguisht Tongue,
Which mine ear kindled into living Word.

91

Said one among them—'Surely not in vain,
My Substance from the common Earth was ta'en,
  That He who subtly wrought me into Shape
Should stamp me back to shapeless Earth again?'

92

Another said, 'Why, ne'er a peevish Boy
Would break the Cup from which he drank in Joy;
  Shall He that of his own free Fancy made
The Vessel, in an after-rage destroy!'

93

None answer'd this; but after silence spake
Some Vessel of a more ungainly Make;
  'They sneer at me for leaning all awry;
What! did the Hand then of the Potter shake?'

94

Thus with the Dead as with the Living, *What?*
And *Why?* so ready, but the *Wherefor* not,
　One on a sudden peevishly exclaim'd,
'Which is the Potter, pray, and which the Pot?'

95

Said one—'Folks of a surly Master tell,
And daub his Visage with the Smoke of Hell;
　They talk of some sharp Trial of us—Pish!
He's a good Fellow, and 'twill all be well.'

96

'Well,' said another, 'Whoso will, let try,
My Clay with long Oblivion is gone dry:
　But fill me with the old familiar Juice,
Methinks I might recover by-and-bye!'

97

So while the Vessels one by one were speaking,
One spied the little Crescent all were seeking:
　And then they jogg'd each other, 'Brother! Brother!
Now for the Porter's shoulder-knot a-creaking!'

✳ ✳ ✳ ✳ ✳ ✳ ✳ ✳

98

Ah, with the Grape my fading Life provide,
And wash my Body whence the Life has died,
   And lay me, shrouded in the living Leaf,
By some not unfrequented Garden-side.

99

Whither resorting from the vernal Heat
Shall Old Acquaintance Old Acquaintance greet,
   Under the Branch that leans above the Wall
To shed his Blossom over head and feet.

100

Then ev'n my buried Ashes such a snare
Of Vintage shall fling up into the Air,
   As not a True-believer passing by
But shall be overtaken unaware.

101

Indeed the Idols I have loved so long
Have done my credit in Men's eye much wrong:
   Have drown'd my Glory in a shallow Cup,
And sold my Reputation for a Song.

102

Indeed, indeed, Repentance oft before
I swore—but was I sober when I swore?
   And then and then came Spring, and Rose-in-hand
My thread-bare Penitence apieces tore.

103

And much as Wine has play'd the Infidel,
And robb'd me of my Robe of Honour—Well,
    I often wonder what the Vintners buy
One half so precious as the ware they sell.

104

Yet Ah, that Spring should vanish with the Rose!
That Youth's sweet-scented manuscript should close!
    The Nightingale that in the branches sang,
Ah whence, and whither flown again, who knows!

105

Would but the Desert of the Fountain yield
One glimpse—if dimly, yet indeed, reveal'd,
    Toward which the fainting Traveller might spring,
As springs the trampled herbage of the field!

106

Oh if the World were but to re-create,
That we might catch ere closed the Book of Fate,
    And make The Writer on a fairer leaf
Inscribe our names, or quite obliterate!

107

Better, oh better, cancel from the Scroll
Of Universe one luckless Human Soul,
    Than drop by drop enlarge the Flood that rolls
Hoarser with Anguish as the Ages roll.

108

Ah Love! could you and I with Fate conspire
To grasp this sorry Scheme of Things entire,
    Would not we shatter it to bits—and then
Re-mould it nearer to the Heart's Desire!

109

But see! The rising Moon of Heav'n again
Looks for us, Sweet-heart, through the quivering Plane:
    How oft hereafter rising will she look
Among those leaves—for one of us in vain!

110

And when Yourself with silver Foot shall pass
Among the Guests Star-scatter'd on the Grass,
    And in your joyous errand reach the spot
Where I made One—turn down an empty Glass!

TAMÁM

NOTES*

(2) The *'False Dawn'*; *Subhi Kázib*, a transient Light on the Horizon about an hour before the *Subhi sâdik*, or True Dawn; a well known Phenomenon in the East.

(4) New Year. Beginning with the Vernal Equinox, it must be remembered; and (howsoever the old Solar Year is practically superseded by the clumsy *Lunar* Year that dates from the Mohammedan Hijra) still commemorated by a Festival that is said to have been appointed by the very Jamshyd whom Omar so often talks of, and whose yearly Calendar he helped to rectify.

'The sudden approach and rapid advance of the Spring,' says Mr. Binning, 'are very striking. Before the Snow is well off the Ground, the Trees burst into Blossom, and the Flowers start forth from the Soil. At *Naw Rooz* (*their* New Year's Day) the Snow was lying in patches on the Hills and in the shaded Vallies, while the Fruit-trees in the Garden were budding beautifully, and green Plants and Flowers springing up on the Plains on every side—

---

* [References are to the stanzas of the second edition.—KS]

> And on old Hyems' Chin and icy Crown
> An odorous Chaplet of sweet Summer buds
> Is, as in mockery, set.— —

Among the Plants newly appear'd I recognized some old Acquaintances I had not seen for many a Year: among these, two varieties of the Thistle; a coarse species of Daisy, like the Horse-gowan; red and white Clover; the Dock; the blue Cornflower; and that vulgar Herb the Dandelion rearing its yellow crest on the Banks of the Watercourses.' The Nightingale was not yet heard, for the Rose was not yet blown: but an almost identical Blackbird and Woodpecker helped to make up something of a North-country Spring.

(4) Exodus iv. 6; where Moses draws forth his Hand—not, according to the Persians, *'leprous as Snow,'*—but *white*, as our May-Blossom in Spring perhaps. According to them also the Healing Power of Jesus resided in his Breath.

(5) Iram, planted by King Schaddád, and now sunk somewhere in the Sands of Arabia. Jamshyd's Seven-ring'd Cup was typical of the 7 Heavens, 7 Planets, 7 Seas, &c., and was a *Divining Cup*.

(6) *Péhlevi*, the old Heroic *Sanskrit* of Persia. Háfiz also speaks of the Nightingale's *Péhlevi*, which did not change with the People's.

(6) I am not sure if this refers to the Red Rose looking sickly, or the Yellow Rose that ought to be Red; Red, White, and Yellow Roses all common in Persia. I

think Southey, in his Common-Place Book, quotes from some Spanish author about a Rose being White till 10 o'clock; 'Rosa perfecta' at 2; and 'perfecta incarnada' at 5.

(10) Rustum, the 'Hercules' of Persia, whose exploits are among the most celebrated in the Sháh-náma. Hátim Tai, a well-known Type of Oriental Generosity.

(13) A Drum—beaten outside a Palace.

(15) That is, the Rose's Golden Centre.

(19) Persepolis: call'd also *Takht'i Jamshyd*—THE THRONE OF JAMSHYD, '*King-Splendid,*' of the mythical *Peeshdádian* Dynasty, and supposed (according to the Sháh-náma) to have been founded and built by him. Others refer it to the Work of the Genie King, Ján Ibn Ján—who also built the Pyramids—before the time of Adam.

BAHRÁM GÚR—*Bahrám of the Wild Ass*—a Sassanian Sovereign—had also his Seven Castles (like the King of Bohemia!) each of a different Colour; each with a Royal Mistress within; each of whom tells him a Story, as told in one of the most famous Poems of Persia, written by Amír Khusraw: all these Sevens also figuring (according to Eastern Mysticism) the Seven Heavens, and perhaps the Book itself that Eighth, into which the mystical Seven transcend, and within which they revolve. The Ruins of Three of these Towers are yet shown by the Peasantry; as also the Swamp in which Bahrám sunk, like the Master of Ravenswood, while pursuing his *Gúr*.

(20) This Quatrain Mr. Binning found, among several of Háfiz and others, inscribed by some stray hand among the ruins of Persepolis. The Ringdove's ancient *Péhlevi, Coo, Coo, Coo,* signifies also in Persian *'Where? Where? Where?'* In Attár's 'Bird-parliament' she is reproved by the Leader of the Birds for sitting still, and for ever harping on that one note of lamentation for her lost Yúsuf.

(21) A thousand years to each Planet.

(24) Satum, Lord of the Seventh Heaven.

(25) ME-AND-THEE: some dividual Existence or Personality distinct from the Whole.

(42) The custom of throwing a little Wine on the ground before drinking still continues in Persia, and perhaps generally in the East. Mons. Nicolas considers it 'un signe de libéralité, et en même temps un avertissement que le buveur doit vider sa coupe jusqu'à la dernière goutte.'* Is it not more likely an ancient Superstition; a Libation to propitiate Earth, or make her an Accomplice in the illicit Revel? Or, perhaps, to divert the Jealous Eye by some sacrifice of superfluity, as with the Ancients of the West? With Omar we see something more is signified; the precious Liquor is not lost, but sinks into the ground to refresh the dust of some poor Wine-worshipper foregone.

---

* ['A sign of liberality, and at the same time a warning that the drinker must empty his cup to the last drop.']

Thus Háfiz, copying Omar in so many ways: 'When thou drinkest Wine pour a draught on the ground. Wherefore fear the Sin which brings to another Gain?'

(46) According to one beautiful Oriental Legend, Azräel accomplishes his mission by holding to the nostril an Apple from the Tree of Life.

(49) The Caravans travelling by night, after the Vernal Equinox—their New Year's Day. This was ordered by Mohammed himself, I believe.

(52) From Máh to Máhi; from Fish to Moon.

(58) A Jest, of course, at his Studies. A curious mathematical Quatrain of Omar's has been pointed out to me; the more curious because almost exactly parallel'd by some Verses of Doctor Donne's, and quoted in Izaak Walton's Lives! Here is Omar: 'You and I are the image of a pair of compasses; though we have two heads (sc. our *feet*) we have one body; when we have fixed the centre for our circle, we bring our heads (sc. feet) together at the end.' Dr. Donne:

> If we be two, we two are so
> As stiff twin-compasses are two;
> Thy Soul, the fixt foot, makes no show
> To move, but does if the other do.
>
> And though thine in the centre sit,
> Yet when my other far does roam,
> Thine leans and hearkens after it,
> And grows erect as mine comes home.

Such thou must be to me, who must
 Like the other foot obliquely run;
Thy firmness makes my circle just,
 And me to end where I begun.

(61) The Seventy-two Religions supposed to divide the World: *including* Islamism, as some think: but others not.

(62) Alluding to Sultan Mahmúd's Conquest of India and its dark people.

(73) *Fánúsi khiyál*, a Magic-lanthorn still used in India; the cylindrical Interior being painted with various Figures, and so lightly poised and ventilated as to revolve round the lighted Candle within.

(75) A very mysterious Line in the Original:

O dánad O dánad O dánad O ——

breaking off something like our Wood-pigeon's Note, which she is said to take up just where she left off.

(81) Parwín and Mushtari—The Pleiads and Jupiter.

(97) At the Close of the Fasting Month, Ramazán (which makes the Musulman unhealthy and unamiable), the first Glimpse of the New Moon (who rules their Division of the Year), is looked for with the utmost Anxiety, and hailed with Acclamation. Then it is that the Porter's Knot may be heard—toward the *Cellar*, perhaps. Omar has elsewhere a pretty Quatrain about the same Moon—

Be of Good Cheer—the sullen Month will die,
And a young Moon requite us by and bye:
　Look how the Old one, meagre, bent, and wan
With Age and Fast, is fainting from the Sky!

RUBÁIYÁT
OF
OMAR KHAYYÁM

FIFTH EDITION

1889

[The fifth edition is essentially the same as the two earlier editions, the third edition of 1872 and the fourth edition of 1879, containing only minor amendments (derived from FitzGerald's notes discovered after his death in 1883). Variations from the fifth edition are indicated in footnotes.]

OMAR KHAYYÁM

THE

ASTRONOMER-POET OF PERSIA

OMAR KHAYYÁM was born at Naishápúr in Khorassán in the latter half of our Eleventh, and died within the First Quarter of our Twelfth Century. The slender Story of his Life is curiously twined about that of two other very considerable Figures in their Time and Country: one of whom tells the Story of all Three. This was Nizám ul Mulk, Vizyr to Alp Arslan the Son, and Malik Shah the Grandson, of Toghrul Beg the Tartar, who had wrested Persia from the feeble Successor of Mahmúd the Great, and founded that Seljukian Dynasty which finally roused Europe into the Crusades. This Nizám ul Mulk, in his *Wasiyat*—or *Testament*—which he wrote and left as a Memorial for future Statesmen—relates the following, as quoted in the *Calcutta Review*, No. 59, from Mirkhond's *History of the Assassins*.

"'One of the greatest of the wise men of Khorassán was the Imám Mowaffak of Naishápúr, a man highly honoured and reverenced—may God rejoice his soul; his illustrious years exceeded eighty-five, and it was the universal belief that every boy who read the Koran or studied the traditions in his presence, would assuredly attain to honour and happiness. For this cause did my father send me from Tús to Naishápúr with Abd-us-samad, the doctor of law, that I might employ myself in study and learning under the guidance of that illustrious teacher. Towards me he ever turned an eye of favour and kindness, and as his pupil I felt for him extreme affection and devotion, so that I passed four years in his service. When I first came there, I found two other pupils of mine own age newly arrived, Hakim Omar Khayyám, and the ill-fated Ben Sabbáh. Both were endowed with sharpness of wit and the highest natural powers; and we three formed a close friendship together. When the Imám rose from his lectures, they used to join me, and we repeated to each other the lessons we had heard. Now Omar was a native of Naishápúr, while Hasan Ben Sabbáh's father was one Ali, a man of austere life and practice, but heretical in his creed and doctrine. One day Hasan said to me and to Khayyám, 'It is a universal belief that the pupils of the Imám Mowaffak will attain to fortune. Now, even if we *all* do not attain thereto, without doubt one of us will; what then shall be our mutual pledge and bond?' We answered, 'Be it what you please.'—'Well,' he said, 'let us make a vow, that to whomsoever this fortune falls, he shall share it equally with the rest, and reserve no pre-eminence for himself.'—'Be it so,' we both replied, and on those terms we mutually pledged our words. Years rolled on, and I went from Khorassán to Transoxiana, and wandered to Ghazni and Cabul; and when I returned, I was invested with office, and rose to be administrator of affairs during the Sultanate of Sultan Alp Arslán."

'He goes on to state, that years passed by, and both his old school-friends found him out, and came and claimed a share in his good fortune, according to the school-day vow. The Vizier was generous and kept his word. Hasan demanded a place in the government, which the Sultan granted at the Vizier's request; but, discontented with a gradual rise, he plunged into the maze of intrigue of an Oriental Court, and, failing in a base attempt to supplant his benefactor, he was disgraced and fell. After many mishaps and wanderings, Hasan became the head of the Persian sect of the *Ismaílians*—a party of fanatics who had long murmured in obscurity, but rose to an evil eminence under the guidance of his strong and evil will. In AD 1090, he seized the castle of Alamút, in the province of Rúdbar, which lies in the mountainous tract south of the Caspian Sea; and it was from this mountain home he obtained that evil celebrity among the Crusaders as the OLD MAN OF THE MOUNTAINS, and spread terror through the Mohammedan world; and it is yet disputed whether the word *Assassin*, which they have left in the language of modern Europe as their dark memorial, is derived from the *hashish*, or opiate of hemp-leaves (the Indian *bhang*), with which they maddened themselves to the sullen pitch of Oriental desperation, or from the name of the founder of the dynasty, whom we have seen in his quiet collegiate days, at Naishápúr. One of the countless victims of the Assassin's dagger was Nizám ul Mulk himself, the old school-boy friend.[1]

'Omar Khayyám also came to the Vizier to claim his share; but not to ask for title or office. "The greatest boon you can confer on me," he said, "is to let me live in a corner under the shadow of your fortune, to spread wide the advantages of Science, and pray for your long life and prosperity." The Vizier tells us, that, when he found Omar was really sincere in his refusal, he pressed him no further, but granted him a yearly pension of 1200 *mithkáls* of gold, from the treasury of Naishápúr.

'At Naishápúr thus lived and died Omar Khayyám, "busied," adds the Vizier, "in winning knowledge of every kind, and especially in Astronomy, wherein he attained to a very high pre-eminence. Under the Sultanate of Malik Shah, he came to Merv, and obtained great praise for his proficiency in science, and the Sultan showered favours upon him."

'When Malik Shah determined to reform the calendar, Omar was one of the eight learned men employed

---

[1] Some of Omar's Rubáiyát warn us of the danger of Greatness, the instability of Fortune, and while advocating Charity to all Men, recommending us to be too intimate with none. Attár makes Nizám ul Mulk use the very words of his friend Omar [Rub. 28], 'When Nizám ul Mulk was in the Agony (of Death) he said, "Oh God! I am passing away in the hand of the wind."'

to do it; the result was the *Jalálí* era (so called from *Jalál-ud-dín*, one of the king's names)—"a computation of time," says Gibbon, "which surpasses the Julian, and approaches the accuracy of the Gregorian style." He is also the author of some astronomical tables, entitled Zíji-Malikshábí, and the French have lately republished and translated an Arabic Treatise of his on Algebra.

'His Takhallus or poetical name (Khayyám) signifies a Tentmaker, and he is said to have at one time exercised that trade, perhaps before Nizám ul Mulk's generosity raised him to independence. Many Persian poets similarly derive their names from their occupations; thus we have Attár, "a druggist," Assár, "an oil presser," etc.[1] Omar himself alludes to his name in the following whimsical lines:

> "'Khayyám, who stitched the tents of science,
> Has fallen in grief's furnace and been suddenly burned;
> The shears of Fate have cut the tent ropes of his life,
> And the broker of Hope has sold him for nothing!"

'We have only one more anecdote to give of his Life, and that relates to the close; it is told in the anonymous preface which is sometimes prefixed to his poems; it has been printed in the Persian in the Appendix to Hyde's

---

[1] Though all these, like our Smiths, Archers, Millers, Fletchers, etc., may simply retain the Surname of an hereditary calling.

Veterum Persarum Religio, p. 499; and D'Herbelot alludes to it in his Bibliothèque, under *Khiam*:[1]

"'It is written in the chronicles of the ancients that this King of the Wise, Omar Khayyám, died at Naishápúr in the year of the Hegira, 517 (AD 1123); in science he was unrivaled—the very paragon of his age. Khwájah Nizámi of Samarcand, who was one of his pupils, relates the following story: 'I often used to hold conversations with my teacher, Omar Khayyám, in a garden; and one day he said to me, "My tomb shall be in a spot where the north wind may scatter roses over it." I wondered at the words he spake, but I knew that his were no idle words.[2] Years after, when I chanced to revisit Nai-

---

[1] 'Philosophe Musulman qui a vécu en Odeur de Sainteté dans sa Religion, vers la Fin du premier et le Commencement du second Siecle,' ['Muslim philosopher who lived in "Odour of Sanctity" in his religion, towards the end of the first and the beginning of the second centuries.'] no part of which, except the 'Philosophe,' can apply to our Khayyám.

[2] The Rashness of the Words, according to D'Herbelot, consisted in being so opposed to those in the Korán: 'No Man knows where he shall die.'—This story of Omar reminds me of another so naturally—and when one remembers how wide of his humble mark the noble sailor aimed—so pathetically told by Captain Cook—not by Doctor Hawkesworth—in his Second Voyage (i. 374). When leaving Ulietea, 'Oreo's last request was for me to return. When he saw he could not obtain that promise, he asked the name of my *Marai* (burying-place). As strange a question as this was, I hesitated not a moment to tell him "Stepney"; the parish in which I live when in London. I was made to repeat it several times over till they could pronounce it; and then "Stepney Marai no Toote" was echoed

shápúr, I went to his final resting-place, and lo! it was just outside a garden, and trees laden with fruit stretched their boughs over the garden wall, and dropped their flowers upon his tomb, so that the stone was hidden under them.'"'

Thus far—without fear of Trespass—from the *Calcutta Review*. The writer of it, on reading in India this story of Omar's Grave, was reminded, he says, of Cicero's Account of finding Archimedes' Tomb at Syracuse, buried in grass and weeds. I think Thorwaldsen desired to have roses grow over him; a wish religiously fulfilled for him to the present day, I believe. However, to return to Omar.

Though the Sultan 'shower'd Favours upon him,' Omar's Epicurean Audacity of Thought and Speech caused him to be regarded askance in his own Time and Country. He is said to have been especially hated and dreaded by the Súfis, whose Practice he ridiculed, and whose Faith amounts to little more than his own, when stript of the Mysticism and formal recognition of Islamism under which Omar would not hide. Their Poets, including Háfiz, who are (with the exception of Firdausi) the most considerable in Persia, borrowed largely, indeed, of Omar's material, but turning it to a

---

through an hundred mouths at once. I afterwards found the same question had been put to Mr. Forster by a man on shore; but he gave a different, and indeed more proper answer, by saying, "No man who used the sea could say where he should be buried."'

mystical Use more convenient to Themselves and the People they addressed; a People quite as quick of Doubt as of Belief; as keen of Bodily Sense as of Intellectual; and delighting in a cloudy composition of both, in which they could float luxuriously between Heaven and Earth, and this World and the Next, on the wings of a poetical expression, that might serve indifferently for either. Omar was too honest of Heart as well as of Head for this. Having failed (however mistakenly) of finding any Providence but Destiny, and any World but This, he set about making the most of it; preferring rather to soothe the Soul through the Senses into Acquiescence with Things as he saw them, than to perplex it with vain disquietude after what they *might* be. It has been seen, however, that his Worldly Ambition was not exorbitant; and he very likely takes a humorous or perverse pleasure in exalting the gratification of Sense above that of the Intellect, in which he must have taken great delight, although it failed to answer the Questions in which he, in common with all men, was most vitally interested.

For whatever Reason, however, Omar, as before said, has never been popular in his own Country, and therefore has been but scantily transmitted abroad. The MSS. of his Poems, mutilated beyond the average Casualties of Oriental Transcription, are so rare in the East as scarce to have reacht Westward at all, in spite of all the acquisitions of Arms and Science. There is no copy at the India House, none at the Bibliothèque Nationale of Paris. We know but of one in England: No. 140 of the

Ouseley MSS. at the Bodleian, written at Shiráz, AD 1460. This contains but 158 Rubáiyát. One in the Asiatic Society's Library at Calcutta (of which we have a Copy) contains (and yet incomplete) 516, though swelled to that by all kinds of Repetition and Corruption. So Von Hammer speaks of *his* Copy as containing about 200, while Dr. Sprenger catalogues the Lucknow MS. at double that number.[1] The Scribes, too, of the Oxford and Calcutta MSS. seem to do their Work under a sort of Protest; each beginning with a Tetrastich (whether genuine or not), taken out of its alphabetical order; the Oxford with one of Apology; the Calcutta with one of Expostulation, supposed (says a Notice prefixed to the MS.) to have arisen from a Dream, in which Omar's mother asked about his future fate. It may be rendered thus:

> Oh Thou who burn'st in Heart for those who burn
> In Hell, whose fires thyself shall feed in turn;
> How long be crying, 'Mercy on them, God!'
> Why, who art Thou to teach, and He to learn?

The Bodleian Quatrain pleads Pantheism by way of Justification.

---

[1] 'Since this paper was written' (adds the Reviewer in a note), 'we have met with a Copy of a very rare Edition, printed at Calcutta in 1836. This contains 438 Tetrastichs, with an Appendix containing 54 others not found in some MSS.'

>If I myself upon a looser Creed
>Have loosely strung the Jewel of Good deed,
>>Let this one thing for my Atonement plead:
>That One for Two I never did mis-read.

The Reviewer,[1] to whom I owe the Particulars of Omar's Life, concludes his Review by comparing him with Lucretius, both as to natural Temper and Genius, and as acted upon by the Circumstances in which he lived. Both indeed were men of subtle, strong, and cultivated Intellect, fine Imagination, and Hearts passionate for Truth and Justice; who justly revolted from their Country's false Religion, and false, or foolish, Devotion to it; but who fell short of replacing what they subverted by such better *Hope* as others, with no better Revelation to guide them, had yet made a Law to themselves. Lucretius, indeed, with such material as Epicurus furnished, satisfied himself with the theory of a vast machine fortuitously constructed, and acting by a Law that implied no Legislator; and so composing himself into a Stoical rather than Epicurean severity of Attitude, sat down to contemplate the mechanical Drama of the Universe which he was part Actor in; himself and all about him (as in his own sublime description of the Roman Theatre) discoloured with the lurid reflex of the Curtain suspended between the Spectator and the Sun. Omar, more desperate, or more careless of any so complicated

---

[1] Professor Cowell.

System as resulted in nothing but hopeless Necessity, flung his own Genius and Learning with a bitter or humorous jest into the general Ruin which their insufficient glimpses only served to reveal; and, pretending sensual pleasure as the serious purpose of Life, only *diverted* himself with speculative problems of Deity, Destiny, Matter and Spirit, Good and Evil, and other such questions, easier to start than to run down, and the pursuit of which becomes a very weary sport at last!

With regard to the present Translation. The original Rubáiyát (as, missing an Arabic Guttural, these *Tetrastichs* are more musically called) are independent Stanzas, consisting each of four Lines of equal, though varied, Prosody; sometimes *all* rhyming, but oftener (as here imitated) the third line a blank. Somewhat as in the Greek Alcaic, where the penultimate line seems to lift and suspend the Wave that falls over in the last. As usual with such kind of Oriental Verse, the Rubáiyát follow one another according to Alphabetic Rhyme—a strange succession of Grave and Gay. Those here selected are strung into something of an Eclogue, with perhaps a less than equal proportion of the 'Drink and make-merry,' which (genuine or not) recurs over-frequently in the Original. Either way; the Result is sad enough: saddest perhaps when most ostentatiously merry: more apt to move Sorrow than Anger toward the old Tentmaker, who, after vainly endeavouring to unshackle his Steps from Destiny, and to catch some authentic Glimpse of TO-MORROW, fell back upon TO-

DAY (which has outlasted so many To-morrows!) as the only Ground he had got to stand upon, however momentarily slipping from under his Feet.

[*The following text was included in the third and fifth editions (but not the fourth, whose Preface concludes at this point), having already appeared in the second edition with slight differences amounting to quoting Nicolas's French text at somewhat greater length.*]

While the second Edition of this version of Omar was preparing, Monsieur Nicolas, French Consul at Resht, published a very careful and very good Edition of the Text, from a lithograph copy at Teheran, comprising 464 Rubáiyát, with translation and notes of his own.

Mons. Nicolas, whose Edition has reminded me of several things, and instructed me in others, does not consider Omar to be the material Epicurean that I have literally taken him for, but a Mystic, shadowing the Deity under the figure of Wine, Wine-bearer, etc., as Háfiz is supposed to do; in short, a Súfi Poet like Háfiz and the rest.

I cannot see reason to alter my opinion, formed as it was more than a dozen years ago[1] when Omar was first shown me by one to whom I am indebted for all I know of Oriental, and very much of other, literature. He admired Omar's Genius so much, that he would gladly have adopted any such Interpretation of his meaning as Mons. Nicolas's if he could.[2] That he could not, appears by his Paper in the *Calcutta Review* already so largely quoted; in which he argues from the Poems themselves, as well as from what records remain of the Poet's Life.

And if more were needed to disprove Mons. Nicolas's Theory, there is the Biographical Notice which he himself has drawn up in direct contradiction to the Interpretation of the Poems given in his Notes. (See pp. 13–14 of his Preface.) Indeed I hardly knew poor Omar was so far gone till his Apologist informed me. For here we see that, whatever were the Wine that Háfiz drank and sang, the veritable Juice of the Grape it was which Omar used, not only when carousing with his friends, but (says Mons. Nicolas) in order to excite himself to that pitch of Devotion which others reached by cries and 'hurlemens.' And yet, whenever Wine, Wine-bearer, etc., occur in the Text—which is often enough—Mons. Nicolas carefully annotates 'Dieu,' 'La Divinité,' etc.: so carefully indeed that one is tempted to think that he

---

[1] [This was written in 1868.—William Aldis Wright]

[2] Perhaps would have edited the Poems himself some years ago. He may now as little approve of my Version on one side, as of Mons. Nicolas's Theory on the other.

was indoctrinated by the Súfi with whom he read the Poems. (Note to Rub. ii. p. 8.) A Persian would naturally wish to vindicate a distinguished Countryman; and a Súfi to enrol him in his own sect, which already comprises all the chief Poets of Persia.

What historical Authority has Mons. Nicolas to show that Omar gave himself up 'avec passion à l'étude de la philosophie des Soufis'? ['with passion to the study of Súfi philosophy'] (Preface, p. 13.) The Doctrines of Pantheism, Materialism, Necessity, etc., were not peculiar to the Súfi; nor to Lucretius before them; nor to Epicurus before him; probably the very original Irreligion of Thinking men from the first; and very likely to be the spontaneous growth of a Philosopher living in an Age of social and political barbarism, under shadow of one of the Two-and-Seventy Religions supposed to divide the world. Von Hammer (according to Sprenger's Oriental Catalogue) speaks of Omar as 'a Free-thinker, and *a great opponent of Sufism;*' perhaps because, while holding much of their Doctrine, he would not pretend to any inconsistent severity of morals. Sir W. Ouseley has written a note to something of the same effect on the fly-leaf of the Bodleian MS. And in two Rubáiyát of Mons. Nicolas's own Edition Súf and Súfi are both disparagingly named.

No doubt many of these Quatrains seem unaccountable unless mystically interpreted; but many more as unaccountable unless literally. Were the Wine spiritual, for instance, how wash the Body with it when dead?

Why make cups of the dead clay to be filled with—'La Divinité'—by some succeeding Mystic? Mons. Nicolas himself is puzzled by some 'bizarres' and 'trop Orientales' ['odd' and 'too Eastern'] allusions and images— 'd'une sensualité quelquefois révoltante' ['a sometimes shocking sensuality'] indeed—which 'les convenances' ['conventions'] do not permit him to translate; but still which the reader cannot but refer to 'La Divinité.'[1] No doubt also many of the Quatrains in the Teheran, as in

---

[1] A Note to Quatrain 234 admits that, however clear the mystical meaning of such Images must be to Europeans, they are not quoted without 'rougissant' ['blushing'] even by laymen in Persia—'Quant aux termes de tendresse qui commencent ce quatrain, comme tant d'autres dans ce recueil, nos lecteurs, habitués maintenant à l'étrangeté des expressions si souvent employées par Khéyam pour rendre ses pensées sur l'amour divin, et à la singularité de ses images trop orientales, d'une sensualité quelquefois révoltante, n'auront pas de peine à se persuader qu'il s'agit de la Divinité, bien que cette conviction soit vivement discutée par les moullahs musulmans, et même par beaucoup de laïques, qui rougissent véritablement d'une pareille licence de leur compatriote à l'égard des choses spirituelles.' ['As for the words of tenderness which begin this quatrain, like so many others in this collection, our readers— now accustomed to the strangeness of the expressions so often employed by Khayyám to convey his thoughts on divine love, to the uniqueness of its too Eastern imagery, of a sensuality that is sometimes shocking—will have no difficulty in persuading themselves that they are about the Godhead, although this interpretation is vigorously debated by Muslim mullahs, and even by many laymen, who readily blush at the licentiousness of their countryman regarding these spiritual things.']

the Calcutta, Copies, are spurious; such *Rubáiyát* being the common form of Epigram in Persia. But this, at best, tells as much one way as another; nay, the Súfi, who may be considered the Scholar and Man of Letters in Persia, would be far more likely than the careless Epicure to interpolate what favours his own view of the Poet. I observed that very few of the more mystical Quatrains are in the Bodleian MS., which must be one of the oldest, as dated at Shiráz, AH 865, AD 1460. And this, I think, especially distinguishes Omar (I cannot help calling him by his—no, not Christian—familiar name) from all other Persian Poets: That, whereas with them the Poet is lost in his Song, the Man in Allegory and Abstraction; we seem to have the Man—the *Bonhomme*—Omar himself, with all his Humours and Passions, as frankly before us as if we were really at Table with him, after the Wine had gone round.

I must say that I, for one, never wholly believed in the Mysticism of Háfiz. It does not appear there was any danger in holding and singing Súfi Pantheism, so long as the Poet made his Salaam to Mohammed at the beginning and end of his Song. Under such conditions Jeláluddín, Jámí, Attár, and others sang; using Wine and Beauty indeed as Images to illustrate, not as a Mask to hide, the Divinity they were celebrating. Perhaps some Allegory less liable to mistake or abuse had been better among so inflammable a People: much more so when, as some think with Háfiz and Omar, the abstract is not only likened to, but identified with, the sensual Image;

hazardous, if not to the Devotee himself, yet to his weaker Brethren; and worse for the Profane in proportion as the Devotion of the Initiated grew warmer. And all for what? To be tantalized with Images of sensual enjoyment which must be renounced if one would approximate a God, who according to the Doctrine, *is* Sensual Matter as well as Spirit, and into whose Universe one expects unconsciously to merge after Death, without hope of any posthumous Beatitude in another world to compensate for all one's self-denial in this. Lucretius's blind Divinity certainly merited, and probably got, as much self-sacrifice as this of the Súfi; and the burden of Omar's Song—if not 'Let us eat'—is assuredly—'Let us drink, for To-morrow we die!' And if Háfiz meant quite otherwise by a similar language, he surely miscalculated when he devoted his Life and Genius to so equivocal a Psalmody as, from his Day to this, has been said and sung by any rather than Spiritual Worshippers.

However, as there is some traditional presumption, and certainly the opinion of some learned men, in favour of Omar's being a Súfi—and even something of a Saint—those who please may so interpret his Wine and Cup-bearer. On the other hand, as there is far more historical certainty of his being a Philosopher, of scientific Insight and Ability far beyond that of the Age and Country he lived in; of such moderate worldly Ambition as becomes a Philosopher, and such moderate wants as rarely satisfy a Debauchee; other readers may be content to believe with me that, while the Wine Omar celebrates is simply the Juice of the Grape, he bragged more than he drank of it, in very defiance perhaps of that Spiritual Wine which left its Votaries sunk in Hypocrisy or Disgust.

RUBÁIYÁT

OF

OMAR KHAYYÁM OF NAISHÁPÚR

1

WAKE ! For the Sun, who scatter'd into flight*
The Stars before him from the Field of Night,†
    Drives Night along with them from Heav'n, and
        strikes
The Sultán's Turret with a Shaft of Light.

---

* The 3rd and 4th editions omit the comma after *Sun*
† In the first draft of the 3rd edition, the 1st and 2nd lines appear:

  Wake! For the Sun before him into Night
  A Signal flung that puts the Stars to flight

[Notes explaining the differences between the 3rd, 4th and 5th editions are adapted from those that appear in *Rubáiyát of Omar Khayyám, Rendered into English Quatrains by Edward FitzGerald* (Boston: L. C. Page, 1899); and are augmented by my efforts in making a detailed comparison of the different editions. Variations from the first two editions may be explored by directly comparing the texts in this current edition, locating parallel stanzas by use of the Table that starts on page 143.—KS]

2

Before the phantom of False morning died,
Methought a Voice within the Tavern cried,
   'When all the Temple is prepared within,
Why nods the drowsy Worshipper outside?'

3

And, as the Cock crew, those who stood before
The Tavern shouted—'Open then the Door!
   You know how little while we have to stay,
And, once departed, may return no more.'

4

Now the New Year reviving old Desires,
The thoughtful Soul to Solitude retires,
   Where the WHITE HAND OF MOSES on the Bough
Puts out, and Jesus from the Ground suspires.

5

Iram indeed is gone with all his Rose,
And Jamshyd's Sev'n-ring'd Cup where no one knows;
   But still a Ruby kindles in the Vine,*
And many a Garden by the Water blows.

---

  * In the 3rd edition this line reads:
    But still a Ruby gushes from the Vine,

6

And David's lips are lockt; but in divine
High-piping Pehleví,* with 'Wine! Wine! Wine!
    Red Wine!'—the Nightingale cries to the Rose
That sallow cheek of hers† to' incarnadine.‡

7

Come, fill the Cup, and in the fire of Spring
Your Winter-garment of Repentance fling:
    The Bird of Time has but a little way
To flutter—and the Bird is on the Wing.

8

Whether at Naishápúr or Babylon,
Whether the Cup with sweet or bitter run,
    The Wine of Life keeps oozing drop by drop,
The Leaves of Life keep falling one by one.

9

Each Morn a thousand Roses brings, you say;
Yes, but where leaves the Rose of Yesterday?
    And this first Summer month that brings the Rose
Shall take Jamshyd and Kaikobád away.

---

* In the 3rd and 4th editions: *Péhlevi,*
† In the 3rd and 4th editions: *her's*
‡ 3rd edition: *to'incarnadine.*

10

Well, let it take them! What have we to do
With Kaikobád the Great, or Kaikhosrú?
    Let Zál and Rustum bluster as they will,*
Or Hátim call to Supper—heed not you.

11

With me along the strip of Herbage strown
That just divides the desert from the sown,
    Where name of Slave and Sultán is forgot—
And Peace to Mahmúd† on his golden Throne!

12

A Book of Verses underneath the Bough,
A Jug of Wine, a Loaf of Bread—and Thou
    Beside me singing in the Wilderness—
Oh, Wilderness were Paradise enow!

13

Some for the Glories of This World; and some
Sigh for the Prophet's Paradise to come;
    Ah, take the Cash, and let the Credit go,
Nor heed the rumble of a distant Drum!

---

* In the 3rd edition:
    Let Zál and Rustum thunder as they will,
† In the 3rd and 4th editions: *Máhmúd*

14

Look to the blowing Rose about us—'Lo,
Laughing,' she says, 'into the world I blow,*
    At once the silken tassel of my Purse
Tear, and its Treasure on the Garden throw.'

15

And those who husbanded the Golden grain,
And those who flung it to the winds like Rain,
    Alike to no such aureate Earth are turn'd
As, buried once, Men want dug up again.

16

The Worldly Hope men set their Hearts upon
Turns Ashes—or it prospers; and anon,
    Like Snow upon the Desert's dusty Face,
Lighting a little hour or two—is gone.†

17

Think, in this batter'd Caravanserai
Whose Portals are alternate Night and Day,
    How Sultán after Sultán with his Pomp
Abode his destined‡ Hour, and went his way.

---

  * These two lines in the 3rd edition transpose the opening quotation mark:

> *Look to the blowing Rose about us—Lo,*
> *'Laughing,' she says, 'into the world I blow,*

† In the 3rd and 4th editions: *was gone.*
‡ In the 3rd and 4th editions: *destin'd*

18

They say the Lion and the Lizard keep
The Courts where Jamshyd gloried and drank deep:*
   And Bahrám, that great Hunter—the Wild Ass
Stamps o'er his Head, but cannot break his Sleep.

19

I sometimes think that never blows so red
The Rose as where some buried Cæsar bled;
   That every Hyacinth the Garden wears
Dropt in her Lap from some once lovely Head.

20

And this reviving Herb whose tender Green
Fledges the River-Lip on which we lean—
   Ah, lean upon it lightly! for who knows
From what once lovely Lip it springs unseen!

21

Ah, my Belovéd, fill the Cup that clears
TO-DAY of past Regrets† and Future Fears:
   To-morrow!—Why, To-morrow I may be
Myself with Yesterday's Sev'n thousand Years.

---

  * In the 3rd edition: *deep;*
  † In the 3rd and 4th editions: *Regret*

22

For some we loved, the loveliest and the best
That from his Vintage rolling Time hath prest,*
    Have drunk their Cup a Round or two before,
And one by one crept silently to rest.

23

And we, that now make merry in the Room
They left, and Summer dresses in new bloom,
    Ourselves must we beneath the Couch of Earth
Descend—ourselves to make a Couch—for whom?

24

Ah, make the most of what we yet may spend,
Before we too into the Dust descend;
    Dust into Dust, and under Dust to lie,†
Sans Wine, sans Song, sans Singer, and—sans End!

25

Alike for those who for TO-DAY prepare,
And those that after some TO-MORROW stare,
    A Muezzín from the Tower of Darkness cries,
'Fools! your Reward is neither Here nor There.'

---

  * In the 3rd edition: *has prest,*
  † In the 3rd and 4th editions:
      Dust into Dust, and under Dust, to lie,

26

Why, all the Saints and Sages who discuss'd
Of the Two Worlds so wisely—they are thrust*
    Like foolish Prophets forth; their Words to Scorn
Are scatter'd, and their Mouths are stopt with Dust.

27

Myself when young did eagerly frequent
Doctor and Saint, and heard great argument
    About it and about: but evermore
Came out by the same door where in I went.

28

With them the seed of Wisdom did I sow,
And with mine own hand† wrought to make it grow;
    And this was all the Harvest that I reap'd—
'I came like Water, and like Wind I go.'

29

Into this Universe, and *Why* not knowing‡
Nor *Whence*, like Water willy-nilly flowing;
    And out of it, as Wind along the Waste,
I know not *Whither*, willy-nilly blowing.

---

* In the 3rd edition this line reads:
    Of the Two Worlds so learnedly are thrust
† In the 3rd edition: *with my own hand*
‡ In the 3rd edition: *knowing,*

30

What, without asking, hither hurried *Whence?*
And, without asking, *Whither* hurried hence!
   Oh, many a Cup of this forbidden Wine
Must drown the memory of that insolence!

31

Up from Earth's Centre through the Seventh Gate
I rose, and on the Throne of Saturn sate;*
   And many a Knot unravel'd by the Road;
But not the Master-knot of Human Fate.

32

There was the Door to which I found no Key;
There was the Veil through which I might not see:†
   Some little talk awhile of Me and Thee
There was—and then no more of Thee and Me.

33

Earth could not answer; nor the Seas that mourn
In flowing Purple, of their Lord forlorn;
   Nor rolling Heaven, with all his Signs reveal'd
And hidden by the sleeve of Night and Morn.

---

* 3rd and 4th editions: *sate,*
† In the 3rd edition: *through which I could not see:*

34

Then of the THEE IN ME who works behind
The Veil, I lifted up my hands to find
   A lamp amid the Darkness; and I heard,
As from Without—'THE ME WITHIN THEE BLIND!'

35

Then to the Lip of this poor earthen Urn
I lean'd, the Secret of my Life to learn:
   And Lip to Lip it murmur'd—'While you live,
Drink!—for, once dead, you never shall return.'

36

I think the Vessel, that with fugitive
Articulation answer'd, once did live,
   And drink; and Ah! the passive Lip I kiss'd,
How many Kisses might it take—and give!

37

For I remember stopping by the way
To watch a Potter thumping his wet Clay:*
   And with its all-obliterated Tongue
It murmur'd—'Gently, Brother, gently, pray!'

---

* 3rd edition: *Clay,*

38*

And has not such a Story from of Old
Down Man's successive generations roll'd
    Of such a clod of saturated Earth
Cast by the Maker into Human mould?

39

And not a drop that from our Cups we throw
For Earth to drink of, but may steal below
    To quench the fire of Anguish in some Eye
There hidden—far beneath, and long ago.

40

As then the Tulip for her morning sup
Of Heav'nly Vintage from the soil looks up,†
    Do you devoutly do the like, till Heav'n
To Earth invert you—like an empty Cup.‡

---

* In the 3rd edition this stanza appears as:

    Listen—a moment listen!—Of the same
    Poor Earth from which that Human Whisper came
        The luckless Mould in which Mankind was cast
    They did compose, and call'd him by the name.

In the first draught of the third edition, the first line of this stanza appears as:

    For, in your Ear a moment—of the same

† In the first draught of the 3rd edition, this line reads:
Of Wine from Heav'n her little Tass lifts up,

‡ In the 3rd edition the dash is omitted.

41

Perplext no more with Human or Divine,
To-morrow's tangle to the winds resign,
    And lose your fingers in the tresses of
The Cypress-slender Minister of Wine.

42

And if the Wine you drink, the Lip you press,*
End in what All begins and ends in—Yes;
    Think then you are TO-DAY what YESTERDAY
You were—TO-MORROW you shall not be less.

43

So when that Angel of the darker Drink†
At last shall find you by the river-brink,
    And, offering his Cup, invite your Soul
Forth to your Lips to quaff—you shall not shrink.

44

Why, if the Soul can fling the Dust aside,
And naked on the Air of Heaven ride,
    Were't not a Shame—were't not a Shame for him‡
In this clay carcase crippled to abide?

---

* In the first draft of the 3rd edition this line reads:
    And if the Cup, and if the Lip you press,

† The 3rd and 4th editions have: *So when the Angel*

‡ The 3rd and 4th editions have:
    Wer't not a Shame—wer't not a Shame for him

45

'Tis but a Tent where takes his one day's rest
A Sultán* to the realm of Death addrest;
 The Sultán* rises, and the dark Ferrásh
Strikes, and prepares it for another Guest.

46

And fear not lest Existence closing your
Account, and mine, should know the like no more;
 The Eternal Sáki from that Bowl has pour'd
Millions of Bubbles like us, and will pour.

47

When You and I behind the Veil are past,
Oh, but the long, long while the World shall last,†
 Which of our Coming and Departure heeds
As the Sea's self should heed a pebble-cast.‡

---

* In the 3rd edition: *Sultan*
† This line in the 3rd edition reads:
 Oh but the long long while the World shall last,
‡ In the 3rd edition this line is typeset:
 As the Sev'n Seas should heed a pebble-cast.

48

A Moment's Halt—a momentary taste
Of BEING from the Well amid the Waste—
　　And Lo!—the phantom Caravan has reach'd*
The NOTHING it set out from—Oh, make haste!

49

Would you that spangle of Existence spend
About THE SECRET—quick about it, Friend!
　　A Hair perhaps divides the False and True—
And upon what, prithee, may life depend?†

50

A Hair perhaps divides the False and True;
Yes; and a single Alif were the clue—
　　Could you but find it—to the Treasure-house,
And peradventure to THE MASTER too;

51

Whose secret Presence, through Creation's veins
Running Quicksilver-like eludes your pains;
　　Taking all shapes from Máh to Máhi; and
They change and perish all—but He remains;

---

* In the 4th edition: *reacht*
　In the first draught of the 3rd edition this line reads:
　　Before the starting Caravan has reach'd
† The 3rd edition has: *does life depend?*

52

A moment guess'd—then back behind the Fold
Immerst of Darkness round the Drama roll'd
    Which, for the Pastime of Eternity,
He doth* Himself contrive, enact, behold.

53

But if in vain, down on the stubborn floor
Of Earth, and up to Heav'n's unopening Door,
    You gaze TO-DAY, while You are You—how then
TO-MORROW, You when shall be You no more?

54

Waste not your Hour, nor in the vain pursuit
Of This and That endeavour and dispute;
    Better be jocund with the fruitful Grape
Than sadden after none, or bitter, Fruit.

55

You know, my Friends, with what a brave Carouse
I made a Second Marriage in my house;
    Divorced old barren Reason from my Bed,
And took the Daughter of the Vine to Spouse.

---

* 3rd edition: *does*

56

For 'Is' and 'Is-not' though with Rule and Line*
And 'Up-and-down' by Logic I define,†
    Of all that one should care to fathom, I
Was never deep in anything but—Wine.

57

Ah, but my Computations, People say,
Reduced the Year to better reckoning?—Nay,
    'Twas only striking from the Calendar
Unborn To-morrow, and dead Yesterday.

58

And lately, by the Tavern Door agape,
Came shining through the Dusk an Angel Shape
    Bearing a Vessel on his Shoulder; and
He bid me taste of it; and 'twas—the Grape!

59

The Grape that can with Logic absolute
The Two-and-Seventy jarring Sects confute:
    The sovereign Alchemist that in a trice
Life's leaden metal into Gold transmute:

---

* 3rd and 4th editions: *Line,*
† 3rd edition: *define*

60

The mighty Mahmúd, Allah-breathing Lord,
That all the misbelieving and black Horde
    Of Fears and Sorrows that infest the Soul
Scatters before him with his whirlwind Sword.

61

Why, be this Juice the growth of God, who dare
Blaspheme the twisted tendril as a Snare?
    A Blessing, we should use it, should we not?
And if a Curse—why, then, Who set it there?

62

I must abjure the Balm of Life, I must,
Scared by some After-reckoning ta'en on trust,
    Or lured with Hope of some Diviner Drink,
To fill the Cup—when crumbled into Dust!

63

Oh threats of Hell and Hopes of Paradise!
One thing at least is certain—*This* Life flies;
    One thing is certain and the rest is Lies;
The Flower that once has blown for ever dies.

64

Strange, is it not? that of the myriads who
Before us pass'd the door of Darkness through,*
   Not one returns to tell us of the Road,
Which to discover we must travel too.

65

The Revelations of Devout and Learn'd
Who rose before us, and as Prophets burn'd,
   Are all but Stories, which, awoke from Sleep
They told their comrades, and to Sleep return'd.†

66

I sent my Soul through the Invisible,
Some letter of that After-life to spell:
   And by and by my Soul return'd to me,
And answer'd 'I Myself am Heav'n and Hell:'

67

Heav'n but the Vision of fulfill'd Desire,
And Hell the Shadow from a Soul on fire,‡
   Cast on the Darkness into which Ourselves,
So late emerged§ from, shall so soon expire.

---

* 3rd edition: *through*
† In the 3rd edition this line reads:
   They told their fellows, and to Sleep return'd.
‡ 4th edition: *fire*
§ 3rd and 4th editions: *emerg'd*

68

We are no other than a moving row
Of Magic Shadow-shapes that come and go
   Round with the Sun-illumined* Lantern held
In Midnight by the Master of the Show;

69

But helpless Pieces of the Game He plays†
Upon this Chequer-board of Nights and Days;
   Hither and thither moves, and checks, and slays,
And one by one back in the Closet lays.

70

The Ball no question makes of Ayes and Noes,
But Here or There as strikes the Player goes;‡
   And He that toss'd you down into the Field,
He knows about it all—HE knows—HE knows!

71

The Moving Finger writes; and, having writ,
Moves on: nor all your Piety nor Wit
   Shall lure it back to cancel half a Line,
Nor all your Tears wash out a Word of it.

---

 * 3rd and 4th editions: *Sun-illumin'd*
 † In the 3rd edition this line reads:

    Impotent Pieces of the Game He plays

 ‡ In the 3rd edition this line reads:

    But Right or Left as strikes the Player goes;

72

And that inverted Bowl they call the Sky,
Whereunder crawling coop'd we live and die,
    Lift not your hands to *It* for help—for It
As impotently moves as you or I.*

73

With Earth's first Clay They did the Last Man knead,
And there of the Last Harvest sow'd the Seed:
    And the first Morning of Creation wrote
What the Last Dawn of Reckoning shall read.

74

YESTERDAY *This* Day's Madness did prepare;
TO-MORROW'S Silence, Triumph, or Despair:
    Drink! for you know not whence you came, nor why:
Drink! for you know not why you go, nor where.

75

I tell you this—When, started from the Goal,
Over the flaming shoulders of the Foal
    Of Heav'n Parwín and Mushtarí[†] they flung,
In my predestined[‡] Plot of Dust and Soul[§]

---

* In the 3rd edition this line reads:

    As impotently rolls as you or I.

† 3rd edition: *Mushtari*
‡ 3rd and 4th editions: *predestin'd*
§ 3rd edition: *Soul.*

76

The Vine had struck a fibre: which about
If clings my Being—let the Dervish flout;
　Of my Base metal may be filed a Key,
That shall unlock the Door he howls without.

77

And this I know: whether the one True Light
Kindle to Love, or Wrath-consume me quite,
　One Flash of It within the Tavern caught
Better than in the Temple lost outright.

78

What! out of senseless Nothing to provoke
A conscious Something to resent the yoke
　Of unpermitted Pleasure, under pain
Of Everlasting Penalties, if broke!

79

What! from his helpless Creature be repaid
Pure Gold for what he lent him* dross-allay'd—
　Sue for a Debt he† never did contract,
And cannot answer—Oh the sorry trade!

---

* 3rd edition: *us*
† 3rd and 4th editions: *we*

80

Oh, Thou,* who didst with pitfall and with gin
Beset the Road I was to wander in,
    Thou wilt not with Predestined† Evil round
Enmesh, and then impute my Fall to Sin!

81

Oh Thou, who Man of baser Earth didst make,
And ev'n with Paradise devise the Snake:
    For all the Sin wherewith the Face of Man
Is blacken'd—Man's forgiveness give—and take!

* * * * * * * *

82

As under cover of departing Day
Slunk hunger-stricken Ramazán away,
    Once more within the Potter's house alone
I stood, surrounded by the Shapes of Clay.

83

Shapes of all Sorts and Sizes, great and small,
That stood along the floor and by the wall;
    And some loquacious Vessels were; and some
Listen'd perhaps, but never talk'd at all.

---

  * 3rd and 4th editions: *Oh Thou,*
  † 3rd and 4th editions: *Predestin'd*

84

Said one among them—'Surely not in vain
My substance of the common Earth was ta'en
    And to this Figure moulded, to be broke,
Or trampled back to shapeless Earth again.'

85

Then said a Second—'Ne'er a peevish Boy
Would break the Bowl from which he drank in joy;
    And He that with his hand the Vessel made
Will surely not in after Wrath destroy.'

86

After a momentary silence spake
Some Vessel of a more ungainly Make;
    'They sneer at me for leaning all awry:
What! did the Hand then of the Potter shake?'

87

Whereat some one of the loquacious Lot—
I think a Súfi pipkin—waxing hot—
    'All this of Pot and Potter—Tell me, then,
'Who is the Potter, pray, and who the Pot?'*

---

  * This line in the 3rd edition reads:
      'Who makes—Who sells—Who buys—Who is the Pot?'

88

'Why,' said another, 'Some there are who tell
Of one who threatens he will toss to Hell
  The luckless Pots he marr'd in making—Pish!
He's a Good Fellow, and 't will all be well.'

89

'Well,' murmur'd one, 'Let whoso make or buy,
My Clay with long Oblivion is gone dry:
  But fill me with the old familiar Juice,
Methinks I might recover by and by.'

90

So while the Vessels one by one were speaking,
The little Moon look'd in that all were seeking:
  And then they jogg'd each other, 'Brother! Brother!
Now for the Porter's shoulder-knot a-creaking!'

91*

Ah, with the Grape my fading Life provide,
And wash the Body whence the Life has died,
  And lay me, shrouded in the living Leaf,
By some not unfrequented Garden-side.

---

* The 3rd and 4th editions interpose a line of asterisks before stanza 91 to indicate the ending of the section featuring the pots. The asterisks have been misplaced it seems, appearing in the 5th edition after stanza 99 (where they also appear in the 3rd and 4th editions for a third time), where apparently they have no function.

92

That ev'n my buried Ashes such a snare
Of Vintage shall fling up into the Air
    As not a True-believer passing by
But shall be overtaken unaware.

93

Indeed the Idols I have loved so long
Have done my credit in this World much wrong:*
    Have drown'd my Glory in a shallow Cup†
And sold my Reputation for a Song.

94

Indeed, indeed, Repentance oft before
I swore—but was I sober when I swore?
    And then and then came Spring, and Rose-in-hand
My thread-bare Penitence apieces tore.

95

And much as Wine has play'd the Infidel,
And robb'd me of my Robe of Honour—Well,
    I wonder often what the Vintners buy
One half so precious as the stuff they sell.

---

* In the 3rd edition this line reads:
    Have done my credit in Men's eye much wrong:
† 3rd and 4th editions: *Cup,*

96

Yet Ah, that Spring should vanish with the Rose!
That Youth's sweet-scented manuscript should close!
    The Nightingale that in the branches sang,
Ah whence, and whither flown again, who knows!

97

Would but the Desert of the Fountain yield
One glimpse—if dimly, yet indeed, reveal'd,
    To which the fainting Traveller might spring,
As springs the trampled herbage of the field!

98

Would but some wingéd Angel ere too late
Arrest the yet unfolded Roll of Fate,
    And make the stern Recorder otherwise
Enregister, or quite obliterate!

99

Ah Love! could you and I with Him conspire
To grasp this sorry Scheme of Things entire,
    Would not we shatter it to bits—and then
Re-mould it nearer to the Heart's Desire!

✳ ✳ ✳ ✳ ✳ ✳ ✳ ✳

100

Yon rising Moon that looks for us again—
How oft hereafter will she wax and wane;
    How oft hereafter rising look for us
Through this same Garden—and for *one* in vain!

101

And when like her, oh Sákí,* you shall pass
Among the Guests Star-scatter'd on the Grass,
    And in your joyous errand reach the spot†
Where I made One—turn down an empty Glass!

TAMÁM

---

* 3rd edition: *Sáki,*
† In the 3rd edition this line reads:
    And in your blissful errand reach the spot

NOTES*

(2) The *'False Dawn'*; *Subhi Kázib*, a transient Light on the Horizon about an hour before the *Subhi sádik*, or True Dawn; a well-known Phenomenon in the East.

(4) New Year. Beginning with the Vernal Equinox, it must be remembered; and (howsoever the old Solar Year is practically superseded by the clumsy *Lunar* Year that dates from the Mohammedan Hijra) still commemorated by a Festival that is said to have been appointed by the very Jamshyd whom Omar so often talks of, and whose yearly Calendar he helped to rectify.

'The sudden approach and rapid advance of the Spring,' says Mr. Binning,[1] 'are very striking. Before the Snow is well off the Ground, the Trees burst into Blossom, and the Flowers start from the Soil. At *Naw Rooz* (*their* New Year's Day) the Snow was lying in patches on the Hills and in the shaded Vallies, while the Fruit-trees in the Garden were budding beautifully, and green Plants and Flowers springing upon the Plains on every side—

---

* [References are to the stanzas of the fifth edition.—KS]
[1] *Two Years' Travel in Persia*, etc., i. 165.

And on old Hyems' Chin and icy Crown
An odorous Chaplet of sweet Summer buds
Is, as in mockery, set.—

Among the Plants newly appeared I recognised some old Acquaintances I had not seen for many a Year: among these, two varieties of the Thistle—a coarse species of the Daisy like the 'Horse-gowan'—red and white Clover—the Dock—the blue Corn-flower—and that vulgar Herb the Dandelion rearing its yellow crest on the Banks of the Water-courses.' The Nightingale was not yet heard, for the Rose was not yet blown: but an almost identical Blackbird and Woodpecker helped to make up something of a North-country Spring.

'The White Hand of Moses.' Exodus iv. 6; where Moses draws forth his Hand—not, according to the Persians, *'leprous as Snow,'*—but *white*, as our May-blossom in Spring perhaps. According to them also the Healing Power of Jesus resided in His Breath.

(5) Iram, planted by King Shaddád, and now sunk somewhere in the Sands of Arabia. Jamshyd's Seven-ring'd Cup was typical of the 7 Heavens, 7 Planets, 7 Seas, etc., and was a *Divining Cup*.

(6) *Pehleví*, the old Heroic *Sanskrit* of Persia. Háfiz also speaks of the Nightingale's *Pehleví*, which did not change with the People's.

I am not sure if the fourth line refers to the Red Rose looking sickly, or to the Yellow Rose that ought to be Red; Red, White, and Yellow Roses all common in Persia. I think that Southey, in his Common-Place Book, quotes from some Spanish author about the Rose being White till 10 o'clock; 'Rosa Perfecta' at 2; and 'perfecta incarnada' at 5.

(10) Rustum, the 'Hercules' of Persia, and Zál his Father, whose exploits are among the most celebrated in the Sháh-náma. Hátim Tai, a well-known type of Oriental Generosity.

(13) A Drum—beaten outside a Palace.

(14) That is, the Rose's Golden Centre.

(18) Persepolis: call'd also *Takht-i-Jamshyd*—THE THRONE OF JAMSHYD, *'King Splendid,'* of the mythical *Peshdádian* Dynasty, and supposed (according to the Sháh-náma) to have been founded and built by him. Others refer it to the Work of the Genie King, Ján Ibn Ján—who also built the Pyramids—before the time of Adam.

BAHRÁM GÚR—*Bahram of the Wild Ass*—a Sassanian Sovereign—had also his Seven Castles (like the King of Bohemia!) each of a different Colour: each with a Royal Mistress within; each of whom tells him a Story, as told in one of the most famous Poems of Persia, written by Amír Khusraw: all these Sevens also figuring (according to Eastern Mysticism) the Seven Heavens; and perhaps the Book itself that Eighth, into which the mystical Seven transcend, and within which they revolve. The Ruins of Three of those Towers are yet shown by the Peasantry; as also the Swamp in which Bahrám sunk, like the Master of Ravenswood, while pursuing his *Gúr*.

> The Palace that to Heav'n his pillars threw,
> And Kings the forehead on his threshold drew—
>   I saw the solitary Ringdove there,
> And 'Coo, coo, coo,' she cried; and 'Coo, coo, coo.'

This Quatrain Mr. Binning found, among several of Háfiz and others, inscribed by some stray hand among the ruins of Persepolis. The Ringdove's ancient *Pehleví Coo, Coo, Coo,* signifies also in Persian *'Where? Where? Where?'* In Attár's 'Bird-parliament' she is reproved by the Leader of the Birds for sitting still, and for ever harping on that one note of lamentation for her lost Yúsuf.

Apropos of Omar's Red Roses in Stanza 19, I am reminded of an old English Superstition, that our Anemone Pulsatilla, or purple 'Pasque Flower' (which grows plentifully about the Fleam Dyke, near Cambridge), grows only where Danish Blood has been spilt.

(21) A thousand years to each Planet.

(31) Saturn, Lord of the Seventh Heaven.

(32) ME-AND-THEE: some dividual Existence or Personality distinct from the Whole.

(37) One of the Persian Poets—Attár, I think—has a pretty story about this. A thirsty Traveller dips his hand into a Spring of Water to drink from. By-and-by comes another who draws up and drinks from an earthen Bowl, and then departs, leaving his Bowl behind him. The first Traveller takes it up for another draught; but is surprised to find that the same Water which had tasted

sweet from his own hand tastes bitter from the earthen Bowl. But a Voice—from Heaven, I think—tells him the clay from which the Bowl is made was once *Man*; and, into whatever shape renewed, can never lose the bitter flavour of Mortality.

(39) The custom of throwing a little Wine on the ground before drinking still continues in Persia, and perhaps generally in the East. Mons. Nicolas considers it 'un signe de libéralité, et en même temps un avertissement que le buveur doit vider sa coupe jusqu'à la dernière goutte.'* Is it not more likely an ancient Superstition; a Libation to propitiate Earth, or make her an Accomplice in the illicit Revel? Or, perhaps, to divert the Jealous Eye by some sacrifice of superfluity, as with the Ancients of the West? With Omar we see something more is signified; the precious Liquor is not lost, but sinks into the ground to refresh the dust of some poor Wine-worshipper foregone.

Thus Háfiz, copying Omar in so many ways: 'When thou drinkest Wine pour a draught on the ground. Wherefore fear the Sin which brings to another Gain?'

(43) According to one beautiful Oriental Legend, Azräel accomplishes his mission by holding to the nostril an Apple from the Tree of Life.

---

* ['A sign of liberality, and at the same time a warning that the drinker must empty his cup to the last drop.']

This, and the two following Stanzas would have been withdrawn, as somewhat *de trop*, from the Text, but for advice which I least like to disregard.

(51) From Máh to Máhi; from Fish to Moon.

(56) A Jest, of course, at his Studies. A curious mathematical Quatrain of Omar's has been pointed out to me; the more curious because almost exactly parallel'd by some Verses of Doctor Donne's, that are quoted in Izaak Walton's Lives! Here is Omar: 'You and I are the image of a pair of compasses; though we have two heads (sc. our *feet*) we have one body; when we have fixed the centre for our circle, we bring our heads (sc. feet) together at the end.' Dr. Donne:

>   If we be two, we two are so
>   As stiff twin-compasses are two;
>   Thy Soul, the fixt foot, makes no show
>   To move, but does if the other do.
>
>   And though thine in the centre sit,
>   Yet when my other far does roam,
>   Thine leans and hearkens after it,
>   And grows erect as mine comes home.
>
>   Such thou must be to me, who must
>   Like the other foot obliquely run;
>   Thy firmness makes my circle just,
>   And me to end where I begun.

(59) The Seventy-two Religions supposed to divide the World, *including* Islamism, as some think: but others not.

(60) Alluding to Sultan Mahmúd's Conquest of India and its dark people.

(68) *Fánúsi khiyál*, a Magic-lantern still used in India; the cylindrical Interior being painted with various Figures, and so lightly poised and ventilated as to revolve round the lighted Candle within.

(70) A very mysterious Line in the Original:

O dánad O dánad O dánad O——

breaking off something like our Wood-pigeon's Note, which she is said to take up just where she left off.

(75) Parwín and Mushtarí—The Pleiads and Jupiter.

(87) This Relation of Pot and Potter to Man and his Maker figures far and wide in the Literature of the World, from the time of the Hebrew Prophets to the present; when it may finally take the name of 'Pot theism,' by which Mr. Carlyle ridiculed Sterling's 'Pantheism.' *My* Sheikh, whose knowledge flows in from all quarters, writes to me—

'Apropos of old Omar's Pots, did I ever tell you the sentence I found in Bishop Pearson on the Creed? "Thus are we wholly at the disposal of His will, and our present and future condition framed and ordered by His free, but wise and just, decrees. *Hath not the potter power over the clay, of the same lump to make one vessel unto honour, and another unto dishonour?* (Rom. ix. 21.) And can that earth-artificer have a freer power over his *brother potsherd* (both being made of the same metal), than God hath over him, who, by the strange fecundity of His omnipotent power, first made the clay out of nothing, and then him out of that?"'

And again—from a very different quarter—'I had to refer the other day to Aristophanes, and came by chance on a curious Speaking-pot story in the *Vespæ*, which I had quite forgotten.

Φιλοκλέων.   Ἄκουε, μὴ φεῦγ'· ἐν Συβάρει γυνή ποτε
     κατέαξ' ἐχῖνον.   [l. 1435
Κατήγορος.   Ταῦτ' ἐγὼ μαρτύρομαι.
Φι. Οὑχῖνος οὖν ἔχων τιν' ἐπεμαρτύρατο·
  Εἶθ' ἡ Συβαρῖτις εἶπεν, εἰ ναὶ τὰν κόραν
  τὴν μαρτυρίαν ταύτην ἐάσας, ἐν τάχει
  ἐπίδεσμον ἐπρίω, νοῦν ἂν εἶχες πλείονα.

'The Pot calls a bystander to be a witness to his bad treatment. The woman says, "If, by Proserpine, instead of all this 'testifying' (comp. Cuddie and his mother in *Old Mortality!*) you would buy yourself a rivet, it would show more sense in you!" The Scholiast explains *echinus* as ἄγγος τι ἐκ κεράμου.'*

---

* [That is, an earthenware pot.
David Barrett (in *Aristophanes: The Frogs and Other Plays*, London: Penguin 1964, page 90) translates the Greek lines that FitzGerald quotes above, thus:

 PROCLEON: Listen, don't go away. You know about the woman from Sybaris who broke a jug?

One more illustration for the oddity's sake from the *Autobiography of a Cornish Rector*, by the late James Hamley Tregenna. 1871.

'There was one odd Fellow in our Company—he was so like a Figure in the *Pilgrim's Progress* that Richard always called him the "ALLEGORY," with a long white beard—a rare Appendage in those days—and a Face the colour of which seemed to have been baked in, like the Faces one used to see on Earthenware Jugs. In our Country-dialect Earthenware is called "*Clome*"; so the Boys of the Village used to shout out after him—"Go back to the Potter, old Clome-face, and get baked over again." For the "Allegory," though shrewd enough in most things, had the reputation of being "*saift-baked,*" i.e. of weak intellect.'

(90) At the Close of the Fasting Month, Ramazán (which makes the Mussulman unhealthy and unamiable), the first Glimpse of the New Moon (who rules their division of the Year) is looked for with the utmost Anxiety, and hailed with Acclamation. Then it is that the Porter's Knot maybe heard—toward the *Cellar*. Omar has elsewhere a pretty Quatrain about the same Moon—

CITIZEN [*to his friend*]: I call you to witness.
PROCLEON: That's exactly what the jug did. It called a friend to witness. And the woman said, 'If you spent less time calling people to witness, and went out and bought a rivet, you'd be showing more sense.'—KS]

154   RUBÁIYÁT OF OMAR KHAYYÁM

    Be of Good Cheer—the sullen Month will die,
    And a young Moon requite us by and by:
      Look how the Old one, meagre, bent, and wan
    With Age and Fast, is fainting from the Sky!

[*This Note, by William Aldis Wright,* appears at the end of many Macmillan editions of the* Rubáiyát.]

It must be admitted that FitzGerald took great liberties with the original in his version of Omar Khayyám. The first stanza is entirely his own, and in stanza 31† of the fourth edition (36 in the second) he has introduced two lines from Attár (See Letters p. 251). In stanza 81 (fourth edition), writes Professor Cowell, 'There is no original for the line about the snake: I have looked for it in vain in Nicholas; but I have always supposed that the last

---

   * [William Aldis Wright (1831–1914) was FitzGerald's closest friend, and after FitzGerald's death in 1883 took on the task of literary executor, publishing *Letters of Edward FitzGerald* (2 vols, 1894), *Letters of Edward FitzGerald to Fanny Kemble* (1895), *Miscellanies* (1900), *More Letters of Edward FitzGerald* (1901), and *Letters and Literary Remains of Edward FitzGerald* (7 vols, 1902–03, expanding on an earlier 1889 edition of three volumes).—KS]

   † [This typographical error was, it seems, neither spotted nor amended: he means in fact stanza 33.]

line is FitzGerald's mistaken version of Quatr. 236 in Nicholas's ed. which runs thus:

> O thou who knowest the secrets of every one's mind,
> Who graspest every one's hand in the hour of weakness,
> O God, give me repentance and accept my excuses,
> O thou who givest repentance and acceptest the excuses of every one.

'FitzGerald mistook the meaning of *giving* and *accepting* as used here, and so invented his last line out of his own mistake. I wrote to him about it when I was in Calcutta; but he never cared to alter it.'

COMPARATIVE TABLE OF STANZAS

First Edition	Second Edition	Third, Fourth and Fifth Editions
1	1	1
2	2	2
3	3	3
4	4	4
5	5	5
6	6	6
7	7	7
	8	8
8	9	9
9	10	10
10	11	11
11	12	12
12	13	13
	14	
13	15	14
15	16	15
14	17	16
16	18	17
17	19	18
	20	

COMPARATIVE TABLE OF STANZAS

First Edition	Second Edition	Third, Fourth and Fifth Editions
20	21	21
21	22	22
22	23	23
18	24	19
19	25	20
23	26	24
24	27	25
26	28	
25	29	26
27	30	27
28	31	28
29	32	29
30	33	30
31	34	31
32	35	32
	36	33
	37	34
33		
34	38	35
35	39	36
36	40	37
	41	38
37		
	42	39
	43	40
	44	
47	45	42
48	46	43

COMPARATIVE TABLE OF STANZAS

First Edition	Second Edition	Third, Fourth and Fifth Editions
	47	46
	48	47
38	49	48
	50	49
	51	50
	52	51
	53	52
	54	53
	55	41
39	56	54
40	57	55
41	58	56
	59	57
42	60	58
43	61	59
44	62	60
	63	61
	64	62
	65	
	66	63
	67	64
	68	65
	69	44
	70	45
	71	66
	72	67
45		
46	73	68

COMPARATIVE TABLE OF STANZAS

First Edition	Second Edition	Third, Fourth and Fifth Editions
49	74	69
50	75	70
51	76	71
	77	
52	78	72
53	79	73
	80	74
54	81	75
55	82	76
56	83	77
	84	78
	85	79
	86	
57	87	80
58	88	81
59	89	82
	90	83
61	91	84
62	92	85
63	93	86
60	94	87
64	95	88
65	96	89
66	97	90
67	98	91
	99	
68	100	92
69	101	93

COMPARATIVE TABLE OF STANZAS

First Edition	Second Edition	Third, Fourth and Fifth Editions
70	102	94
71	103	95
72	104	96
	105	97
	106	98
	107	
73	108	99
74	109	100
75	110	101

GLOSSARY*

[Terms are located by page numbers for references to Prefaces and Notes, or by edition, stanza, line.]

Alif [*a'-lif*] Name of the first letter in the Persian alphabet; the only vowel written [2.51.2, 5.50.2].

Allah [*al'-lā*] Arabic name for God. The absolute [2.62.1, 5.60.1].

Assár [*as'-sār*] Oil pressers [vii, 33, 103].

Attár [*at'-tār*] Druggist [vii, 33, 103].

Attár [*at'-tār*] A famous Persian Poet, Farrîd-uddîn Attâr, author of the *Mantiq al-Tayr*, (*The Bird Parliament*), partly paraphrased by Edward FitzGerald [vii, 33, 92, 102n.1, 103, 114, 148, 154].

Bahrám Gur [*bah'-rām goor*] Persian king and hunter [20, 61, 91, 147; 1.17.3, 2.19.3, 5.18.3].

---

* This Glossary appears with minor amendments and alterations in several editions of the *Rubáiyát*: this version (revised by the Editor) is taken from *Rubáiyát of Omar Khayyám* (London: Howard Wilford Bell, 1901).

Caravanserai [*kar-a-van'-se-ray*]. An inn where caravans lodge for the night [1.16.1, 2.18.1, 5.17.1].

Dánad [*daw-nad*] 'He knows.' Third person singular of *dán* to know [21, 62, 94, 151].

Fánúsi Khiyál [*fā-noo'-see khee'-yal*] Magic lantern [21, 61, 94, 151].

Ferrásh [*fer-rāsh'*] A servant, tent-pitcher [2.70.3, 5.45.3].

Hátim Tai [*hā'tim tye*] A famous pre-Islamic Arabian poet, famed for his generosity [18, 59, 91, 147; 1.9.4, 2.10.4, 5.10.4].

Hijra, 'Flight', used specifically of the migration of the prophet Muhammad and his followers to the city of Medina in June 622; this is the year from which the Muslim calendar counts [17, 57, 89, 145].

Imám [*i-mām'*] One who leads prayer at Islamic gatherings; used of Imám Mowaffak of Naishápur [iv, 29, 30, 99, 100].

Iram/Irám [*ee'-ram*] The Arabian garden fabled to have been planted by Shaddád bin Ad [58, 90, 146; 1.5.1, 2.5.1, 5.5.1].

Jámí [*jā'-mi*] Persian poet (d. 1492) [114].

Jamshyd/Jamshýd [*jam'-sheed*] A mythical Persian king of the Pishdadian dynasty. According to Firdausi, in his epic work the *Shāhnāmeh*, he reigned 700 years. His palace was at Persepolis [17, 18, 19, 57, 58, 59, 89, 90, 91, 145, 146, 147; 1.5.2, 1.8.4, 1.17.2, 2.5.2, 2.9.4, 2.19.2, 5.5.2, 5.9.4, 5.18.2].

Jeláluddín [*je-lāl'-ud-deen*] Malikshah. A Seljuk sultan (1072–1092) [114].

Kaikhosrú [*kye'-khos-roo*] Mythical Persian King [1.9.2, 2.10.2, 5.10.2].

Kaikobád [*kye'-ko-bād*] A mythical king [1.8.4, 1.9.2, 2.9.4, 2.10.2, 5.9.4, 5.10.2].

Khorassan/Khorassán/Khorássán [*kho-rā-sān'*] The largest of the Persian provinces, a historic region that covered parts of present-day Afghanistan, Iran, Turkmenistan, Uzbekistan and Tajikistan, Khorasan is where Omar Khayyám was born in 1048 [iii, iv, v, 29, 31, 99, 101].

Kúza-Náma [*koo'-za nā'-ma*] 'Book of Pots', title given to stanzas 59–66 in the 1st edition of the *Rubáiyát* [13, 53].

Máh, The moon [93, 150; 2.52.3, 5.51.3].

Máhi, Fish [93, 150; 2.52.3, 5.51.3].

Mahmúd [*mah'-mood*] King of Ghazni, 971–1030. The most prominent ruler of the Ghaznavid dynasty, ruling from 997 until his death in 1030 [iii, 29, 61, 94, 99, 151; 1.10.4, 1.44.1, 2.11.4, 2.62.1, 5.11.4, 5.60.1].

Muezzín [*moo-ez'-zin*] Anglicised from the Arabic word meaning 'he who calls to prayer' [1.24.3, 2.27.3, 5,25,3].

Mushtara/Mushtari/Mushtarí [*mush'-ta-ree*] The planet Jupiter [21, 62, 94, 151; 1.54.3, 2.81.3, 5.75.3].

Naishápur/Naishápúr [*nay'-shā-poor*] In present-day Iran, Nishapur or Neyshabur, the famous city in the region of Khorasan, is where Omar Khayyám was born in 1048 [iii, iv, vi, viii, 29, 30, 32, 34, 99, 100, 102, 104; 2.8.1, 5.8.1].

Naw Rooz/Now Rooz, The Persian New Year's day [17, 57, 89, 145].

Parwín [*par'-ween*] The Pleiades [21, 62, 94, 151; 1.54.3, 2.81.3, 5.75.3].

Péhlevi/Pehleví [*peh'-le-vee*] The principal language of the Persians from the third to the ninth centuries [18, 20, 59, 60, 90, 92, 146, 148; 1.6.2, 2.6.2, 5.6.2].

Ramazán [*ram-a-zān*] The ninth Muslim month, devoted to fasting [21, 62, 94, 153; 1.59.2, 2.89.2, 5.82.2].

Rubáiyát [*roo'-bye-yāt*] Plural of Arabic *rubáiyáh*, a quatrain or stanza of four lines.

Rustum [*rus'-tum*] A mythical Persian hero, son of Zál, and father of Sohráb in the *Shah-náma* [18, 59, 91, 147; 1.9.3, 2.10.3, 5.10.3].

GLOSSARY

Sáki/Sákí [*sā-kee*] A cupbearer [ix, 36; 2.47.3, 5.46.3, 5.101.1].

Shah-náma/Sháh-náma, [*shā-nāma*] *The Book of Kings* or *The Epic of Kings*, by Abul Kasim Mansur, better known as Firdausi (935–1020) [18, 19, 59, 91, 147].

Sheikh [*shaykh*] Arabic Sheekh. An Arabian chief; literally, old man, hence a title of respect; Sheikh-u'l-islam, chief of religion [151].

Subhi Kházib [*soob'-hee kā'-zib*] The false dawn [17, 57, 89, 145].

Subhi Sádik/Subhi Sâdik [*soob'-hee sā'-dik*] The true dawn [17, 57, 89, 145].

Sultan/Sultán [*sul-tān*] King [v, vi, viii, xii, 31, 32, 35, 39, 94, 101, 102, 105, 151; 1.1.4, 1.10.3, 1.10.4, 1.16.3, 2.1.4, 2.11.3, 2.18.3, 2.70.2, 2.70.3, 5.1.4, 5.11.3, 5.17.3, 5.45.2, 5.45.3].

Takhallus [*ta-khal-lus*] Pen-name used by Persian poets; for example, Abul Kasim Mansur, author of the *Shahnama*, called himself Firdausi from Firdaus which means *Paradise*. Omar called himself Khayyám, i.e., Tent-maker [vii, 33, 103].

Tamám [*ta-mām*] The End (all editions excepting the first).

Tamám Shud [*ta-mām' shood*] The Very End (in the first edition only).

Vizier/Vizyr [*vi-zeer'*] A minister or counsellor of state [iii, v, vi, 29, 31, 32, 99, 101, 102].

Zál [*zāl*] The father of Rustum [147; 5.10.3].

Rubáiyát of Omar Khayyám
Translated into English Verse by Edward FitzGerald
Special Facsimile Edition
Edited by Keith Seddon
Published by Lulu 2010
© 2010 Keith Seddon
ISBN 978–1–4457–5638–7 (hardback)
ISBN 978–1–4457–5637–0 (paperback)

Typeset in Iowan Old Style by the editor using Microsoft Word 2007. Proofs checked and reviewed in Portable Document Format created using open source PDFCreator 0.9.9.

NOTE ON THE TYPEFACE

All text is set in Iowan Old Style BT, designed by noted sign painter John Downer.

Iowan Old Style, originally issued in 1991, is a Venetian old style font, modeled after earlier, 20th century American revivals of Italian Renaissance types cut by Nicolas Jenson and Francesco Griffo, but featuring a larger x-height, tighter letterfit and reproportioned capitals. It was also inspired by classical inscriptional lettering as well as sign painting seen in certain regions of eastern Iowa. The Iowan Old Style family was designed for and is well suited for extended use in book text setting.

(Adapted from http://www.bitstream.com/corporate/news/press_2002/type_020313_iowan.html)